Royal Commission on the
Future of the
Toronto Waterfront

Commission royale sur
l'avenir du
secteur riverain de Toronto

Commissioner
The Honourable David Crombie, P.C.

Executive Director and Counsel
Ronald L. Doering

Commissaire
L'honorable David Crombie, c.p.

Directeur exécutif et Conseiller juridique
Ronald L. Doering

Dear Colleague:

I am pleased to provide you with a copy of the report, *East Bayfront and Port Industrial Area: Environment in Transition*. As previously announced, this study is one of the topics for the public hearings on Environment and Health which commence on 22 May 1990. If you wish further information, please contact the offices of the Royal Commission.

This report summarizes the work undertaken during Phase I of an environmental audit of the East Bayfront and Port Industrial Area. It was prepared under the guidance of a steering committee composed of representatives from the federal, provincial and Metropolitan Toronto governments, as well as independent environmental experts. The report represents the collective opinion of the steering committee and provides a preliminary understanding of the environmental conditions of the area which will be further explored during Phase II of the audit.

I look forward to hearing from you.

Cordially,

Cher collègue,

J'ai le plaisir de vous faire parvenir un exemplaire du rapport intitulé, *East Bayfront et le secteur industriel portuaire: un milieu et transition*. Comme nous l'avons déjà annoncé, cette étude fait partie des questions qui seront abordées pendant les audiences publiques sur l'environnement et la santé, qui commenceront le 22 mai 1990. Si vous avez besoin de plus de renseignements, n'hésitez pas à communiquer avec les bureaux de la Commission royale.

Le rapport présente le travail effectué pendant la première étape d'une analyse d'impact des pratiques sur l'environnement du secteur de East Bayfront et du secteur portuaire industriel. Il a été rédigé sous les auspices d'un comité directeur composé de représentants des gouvernements fédéral et provincial et de la communauté urbaine de Toronto, ainsi que d'experts indépendants. Il représente l'opinion collective des membres du comité et donne un aperçu préliminaire des conditions environnementales dans la région, lesquelles seront explorées plus longuement pendant la deuxième étape de l'analyse.

En espérant recevoir bientôt de vos nouvelles, je vous prie d'agréer, cher collègue, l'expression de mes plus cordiales saluations.

David Crombie

171, rue Slater St., 11th Floor/11e étage
P.O. Box/C.P. 1527
Station/Succursale "B"
Ottawa, Canada K1P 6P5

Tel. No./No. de téléphone: *(613)* 990–3306
Fax. No./No. de facsimilé: *(613)* 990–4345

207 Queen's Quay West/Ouest ,5th Floor/5
P.O. Box/ C.P. 4111
Station/Succursale "A"
Toronto, Canada M5W 2V4

Tel. No./No. de téléphone: *(416)* 973–7185
Fax No./No.de facsimilé: *(416)* 973–7103

East Bayfront and Port Industrial Area:

Environment in Transition

A Report on Phase I of an Environmental Audit of Toronto's East Bayfront and Port Industrial Area

The Royal Commission on the Future of the Toronto Waterfront

April 1990

Canadian Cataloguing in Publication Data

Royal Commission on the Future of the Toronto Waterfront (Canada)

Environment in transition: a report on phase I of an environmental audit of Toronto's East Bayfront and Port Industrial Area

ISBN 0–662–17847–5
DSS cat. no. Z1–1988/1–52–3E

1. Environmental auditing — Ontario — Toronto Metropolitan Area. 2. Environmental health — Ontario — Toronto Metropolitan Area. 3. Environmental law — Canada. 4. City planning — Ontario — Toronto Metropolitan Area. I. Title. II. Title: A report on phase I of an environmental audit of Toronto's East Bayfront and port industrial areas.

TD194.7. R69 1990   363.7'009713541   C90–098628–X

Frontispiece

Aerial photograph of a section of the study area illustrating the mix of environments: Lower Don, Gardiner/Lakeshore Corridor, docks and channels, industrial uses, vacant lots and Cherry Beach.

Photo courtesy of the airborne sensing corporation.

Cette publication est aussi disponible en français.

©Minister of Supply and Services Canada 1990
Cat. No. Z1–1988/1–52–3E
ISBN 0–662–17847–5

 recycled paper

TABLE OF CONTENTS

STEERING COMMITTEE AND WORK GROUPS

STEERING COMMITTEE

David Carter (Chair)	Senior Director, Special Projects	Royal Commission on the Future of the Toronto Waterfront
Suzanne Barrett	Co–ordinator, Environmental Audit	Royal Commission on the Future of the Toronto Waterfront
Brian Denney	Manager	Engineering & Development Section, Metropolitan Toronto & Region Conservation Authority
David Egar	Regional Director General	Conservation & Protection, Ontario Region, Environment Canada
Don Gamble	Executive Director	Rawson Academy of Aquatic Science
Lino Grima	Professor	Institute for Environmental Studies, University of Toronto
David Guscott	Director, Central Region	Ontario Ministry of the Environment
Joanna Kidd	Senior Associate	Lura Group
Lynn Morrow	Co–ordinator	Metropolitan Waterfront Committee, Municipality of Metropolitan Toronto
Chuck Pautler	Cabinet Liaison & ResearchCo–ordinator	Office for the Greater Toronto Area
Ron Shimizu	Regional Director of the Great Lakes	Environment Canada

Steering Committee

Alternates

Simon Llewellyn	Manager	Pollution Abatement Division, Environment Canada
Jim Maxwell	Director	Policy Branch: Conservation & Protection, Environment Canada
Bob Shaw	Acting Technical Manager	Ontario Ministry of the Environment
Peter Sly	Director of Science Program	Rawson Academy of Aquatic Science
Mike Thorne	Acting Deputy Commissioner	Metropolitan Works Department, Municipality of Metropolitan Toronto
Rob Tonus	Research Assistant	Conservation Council of Ontario
James Young	Acting Director General Research	Atmospheric Environment Service, Environment Canada

SPECIAL ADVISORS

Andy Hamilton	Senior Environmental Advisor	International Joint Commission
Henry Regier	Professor	Institute for Environmental Studies, University of Toronto

WORK GROUPS

Air

S.M. Daggupaty (Co–Chair)	Research Scientist	Atmospheric Environment Service, Environment Canada
David Yap (Co–Chair)	Supervisor	Air Quality & Meteorology Section, Ontario Ministry of the Environment
Tibor Haasz	Quality Control Officer	Metropolitan Works Department, Municipality of Metropolitan Toronto
P.K. Misra	Manager	Air Quality & Meteorology Section, Ontario Ministry of the Environment
Lou Shenfeld	President	The MEP Company

Built Heritage

Beverly Morley (Chair)	Director, Community Relations	Royal Commission on the Future of the Toronto Waterfront
Adam Carr	Graduate Student	York University
Gene Desfor	Professor	Faculty of Environmental Studies, York University
Morris Fine	Planner	Metropolitan Planning Department, Municipality of Metropolitan Toronto
Richard Stromberg	Manager, Inventory & Research	Toronto Historical Board

Natural Heritage

Suzanne Barrett (Chair)	Environmental Audit	Royal Commission on the Future of the Toronto Waterfront
James Flagal	Articling Student	Osgoode Hall Law School
Beth Jefferson	Chairperson, Records Committee	Toronto Ornithological Club
Karl Konze	Student of Biological Sciences	University of Guelph
Ed Mickiewicz	Planner	Metropolitan Planning Department, Municipality of Metropolitan Toronto

Soils and Groundwater

Paul Beck (Chair)	Senior Hydrogeologist	Intera Kenting
Kevin Hosler	President	KRH Environmental Inc.
Kenneth Raven	Manager, Hydrogeology Group	Intera Technologies Ltd.
Louis Sabourin	Hydrogeologist	Intera Kenting
Dave Trudeau	Chief Project Engineer	Engineering Division, Metropolitan Works Department, Municipality of Metropolitan Toronto

Water

Rob Dobos (Chair)	Surveillance Officer	Great Lakes Water Quality Division, Environment Canada
C.H. Chan	Aquatic Resource Officer	Great Lakes Water Quality Division, Environment Canada
Mike Thorne	Acting Deputy Commissioner	Metropolitan Works Department, Municipality of Metropolitan Toronto

Advisors on Regulatory Framework

Paul Muldoon	Research Associate	Canadian Institute for Environmental Law & Policy
Marcia Valiante	Research Associate	Canadian Institute for Environmental Law & Policy
Burkhard Mausberg	Research Assistant	Canadian Institute for Environmental Law & Policy
Carole Saint Laurent	Research Assistant	Canadian Institute for Envionmental Law & Policy

ACKNOWLEDGEMENTS

ACKNOWLEDGEMENTS

The Environmental Audit of the East Bayfront/Port Industrial Area is being undertaken by the Royal Commission on the Future of the Toronto Waterfront with support from Environment Canada, the Ontario Ministry of the Environment, and the Municipality of Metropolitan Toronto.

This report represents the work of many people. The Steering Committee provided clear guidance to the project as well as prompt reviews of draft manuscripts. The five work groups – on air, water, soils and groundwater, natural heritage, and built heritage – gathered and presented a considerable amount of information in a short time frame (January – March 1990). The work groups received significant input from naturalists, environmentalists, community organizations, government agencies, and industries. The staff at the Royal Commission on the Future of the Toronto Waterfront assisted in many aspects of the study. We thank everyone who contributed during Phase I and look forward to their continuing involvement in Phase II.

INTRODUCTION

This report concludes the first phase of an environmental audit of Toronto's East Bayfront/Port Industrial Area.

It is, in effect, a status report, one source of information on which the Royal Commission on the Future of the Toronto Waterfront can base its public hearings on environmental and health issues, scheduled to begin on 22 May 1990; they are a continuation of earlier hearings held in the spring of 1989.

The audit, which the Royal Commission is leading at the request of the governments of Canada and Ontario, involves substantial intergovernmental co–operation. Both levels of government actively support and participate in the work, as does the Municipality of Metropolitan Toronto and the Metropolitan Toronto and Region Conservation Authority. Several environmental organizations, community groups, and private businesses are also involved in, or have contributed to, the process, and the Royal Commission is grateful to them for their co–operation and assistance.

The City of Toronto was not involved in Phase I of the audit, but will be joining in Phase II. Although it was invited to participate, the Board of Toronto Harbour Commissioners has not done so.

The purpose of the audit is to develop the best possible description and understanding of the environmental conditions of the East Bayfront/Port Industrial Area. On 17 October 1989 the Government of Ontario designated the area as being of Provincial Interest under the *Planning Act*. It did so to protect the integrity of the Royal Commission's studies and to ensure that development that might foreclose future options does not occur during the period of study and related decision–making.

The agreement to undertake the audit represents a positive federal, provincial, and Metropolitan Toronto response to recommendations made by the Royal Commission in its *Interim Report* of August 1989. The Commission recommended "a complete evaluation of all THC lands ... including ... tests of air, water, and soil quality to identify and measure contaminants ... before any major decisions are made on the future of the Port and the lands adjacent to it" (Chapter 3, p. 118). The *Interim Report* also recommended that the Toronto Harbour Commissioners (THC) lands and adjacent provincial lands in the Central Waterfront be pooled "in order to facilitate the necessary degree of co–operation and co–ordination among jurisdictions with an interest in the future of the Toronto waterfront" (Chapter 3, p. 119).

The specific area affected by the declaration of Provincial Interest is bounded on the east by Ashbridge's Bay, on the north by Lakeshore Boulevard East, and on the west by Yonge Street (see Figure 1). It includes all the lands in the East Bayfront/Port Industrial Area down to the water, and the extension of the Leslie Street Spit as far as the northern edge of Tommy Thompson Park: i.e., approximately 567 hectares (1,400 acres). The park itself is not included because it is undergoing an environmental assessment by MTRCA.

This designated area consists entirely of lakefill placed there over successive decades by the THC in implementing its 1912 waterfront plan for building the Port and creating lands for industry, housing, and recreation. Over the years, however, metal–working, fuel and bulk storage, waste transfer, and recycling facilities were constructed; Hydro's coal–burning thermal generating station (now moth–balled) was built; Metro's Main Sewage Treatment Plant and its incinerator (now closed) were operated; and other industrial installations were established. As a result, the area has developed the image of being, in the words of the Royal Commission's *Interim Report*, "a dumping ground for the rest of the City".

Most of the lands are in the hands of the THC, the Province, Metro Toronto, and the City of Toronto. Only 26 properties, representing some 18 per cent of the designated area (370 hectares or 920 acres), are privately owned. There are more than 100 tenants in the area, principally industrial,

FIGURE 1: DESIGNATED AREA

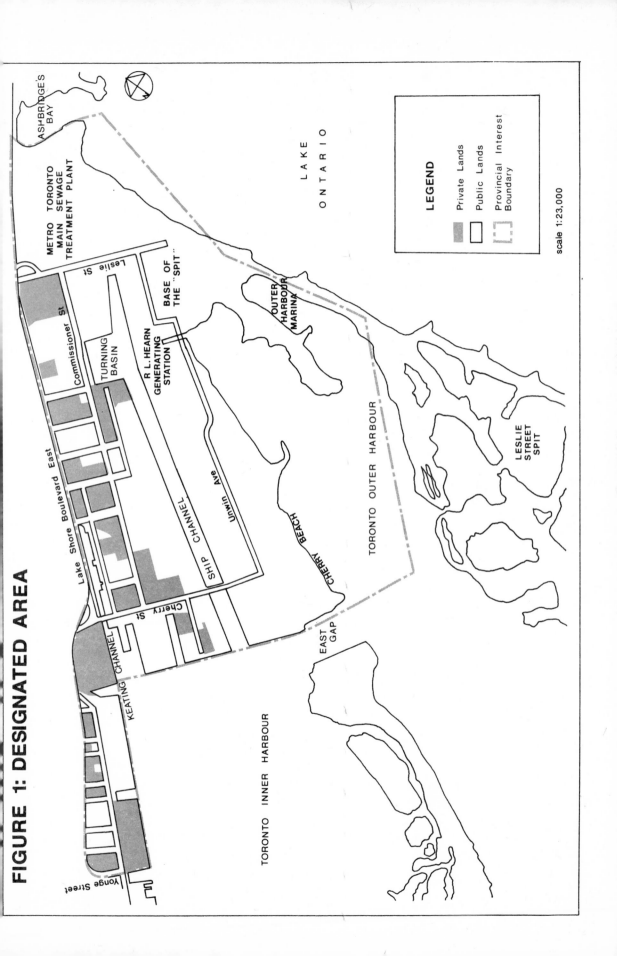

LEGEND

Private Lands
Public Lands
Provincial Interest Boundary

scale 1:23,000

transportation, and commercial enterprises, as well as a small number of recreational organizations.

No people live in the designated area at present. However, there are established neighbourhoods in the vicinity (e.g., South Riverdale, Harbourfront, the Toronto Islands), as well as the proposed Ataratiri development. It is important to recognize that people living in these areas may be affected by existing and future environmental conditions in the East Bayfront/Port Industrial Area.

There are four reasons why the Royal Commission recommended and the governments chose to conduct an environmental audit of the area:

- First, the East Bayfront/Port Industrial Area is in a state of change. The Royal Commission believes that the best way to manage change is to integrate environmental considerations fully into the planning process; this means making a thorough analysis of environmental conditions before any planning is undertaken.

- Second, the designated area is among those parts of the waterfront suffering the greatest environmental stress. This was underlined by the International Joint Commission (IJC) when it declared that the Toronto waterfront is one of 42 "hot spots" around the Great Lakes system — 17 of which are in Ontario. These are places where environmental degradation is deemed to have reached serious dimensions that require specific remedial action.

- Third, the area is strategically located at the centre of the Greater Toronto Area waterfront, minutes from downtown Toronto, and is almost completely in public ownership. It constitutes an appropriate starting point for implementation of the green strategy the Province has asked the Royal Commission to develop for the 135 kilometres of waterfront that stretch between Burlington and Newcastle.

FIGURE 2: GREATER TORONTO AREA

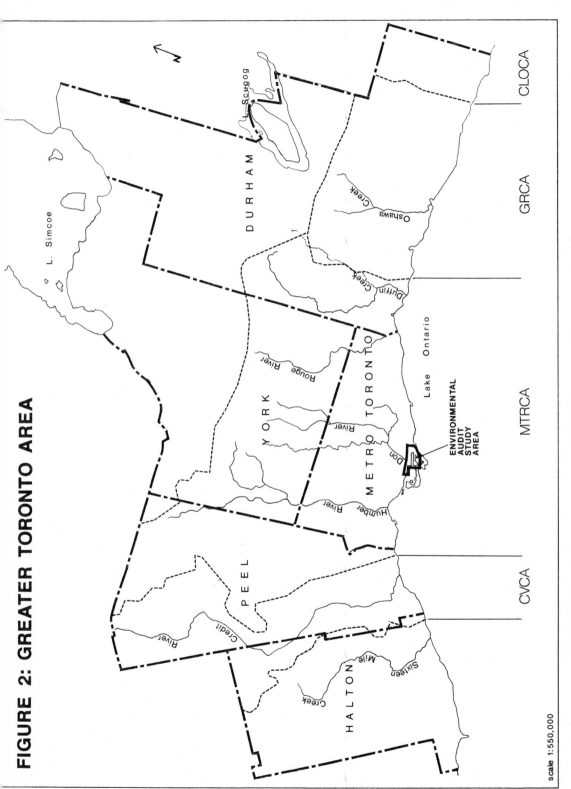

scale 1:550,000

Conservation authorities: Halton Region (HRCA), Credit Valley (CVCA), Metropolitan Toronto & Region (MTRCA), Central Lake Ontario (CLOCA), and Ganaraska Region (GRCA).

- Fourth, the area is situated at the mouth of the Don River and is the link between the waterfront and the Don River valley and watershed. The watershed lies within the boundaries of Metropolitan Toronto, the Regional Municipality of York, and seven municipalities: Toronto, East York, Scarborough, North York, Vaughan, Markham, and Richmond Hill. The fact that the area being studied is at the downstream point of the watershed offers an opportunity to demonstrate the importance of taking a watershed approach to urban and rural planning.

Both the history and the geography of the East Bayfront/ Port Industrial Area dictate that before a green strategy can be developed, before any environmental remediation is implemented, and certainly before any further development or redevelopment of the area occurs, existing environmental conditions must be accurately described, as must the factors that have led to those conditions or that influence them, whether they are internally or externally generated. Hence, the environmental audit.

An audit — rather than an environmental assessment under the *Environmental Assessment Act* — was chosen as the vehicle for studying environmental conditions in the area because of a very important distinction between the two processes:

An environmental assessment is normally carried out by a proponent of a particular development proposal. The assessment judges the environmental impact of the proposed development and alternatives, and determines what, if any, environmental protection, mitigation or remediation will be required if the project is approved. Because assessments are geared to individual projects, they tend not to take into account the cumulative effects of a number of projects.

This environmental audit is not being conducted by a proponent of any particular project but has as its objective the scientific appraisal of conditions in the area to develop the

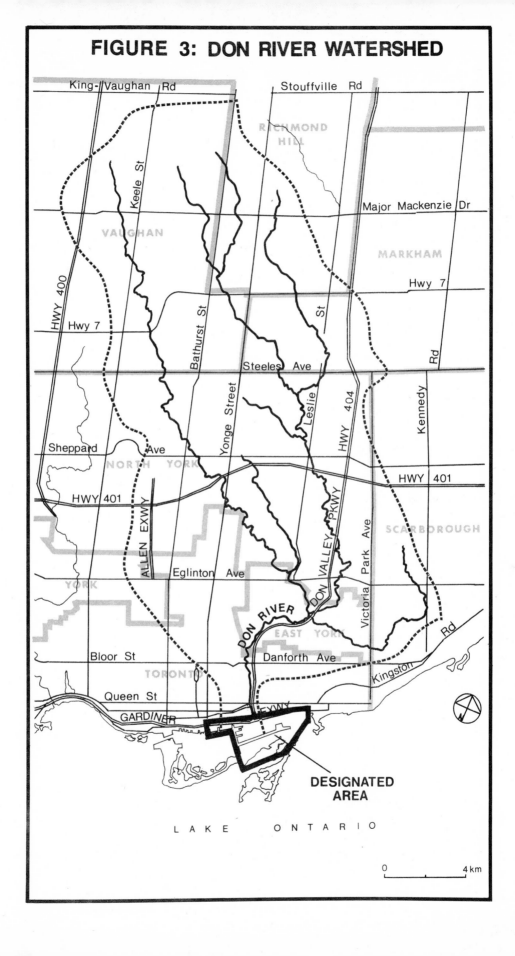

FIGURE 3: DON RIVER WATERSHED

King-Vaughan Rd

Stouffville Rd

RICHMOND HILL

Keele St

Major Mackenzie Dr

VAUGHAN

MARKHAM

HWY 400

Hwy 7

Hwy 7

Bathurst St

St

Steeles Ave

Yonge Street

Leslie

HWY 404

Kennedy Rd

Sheppard Ave

NORTH YORK

HWY 401

HWY 401

ALLEN EXWY

SCARBOROUGH

DON VALLEY PKWY

Eglinton Ave

YORK

Victoria Park Ave

DON RIVER

EAST YORK

Bloor St

Danforth Ave

Kingston Rd

TORONTO

Queen St

GARDINER EXWY

DESIGNATED AREA

LAKE ONTARIO

0   4 km

fullest possible understanding of the environment before any further planning, development or redevelopment occurs. It therefore provides the context for a wide range of options.

The audit approach has tended to open up a different mind set among those involved. Indeed, it has been interesting to note that while, at the beginning, even environmental experts would pose challenges such as, "Tell us what land use you have in mind, and we'll tell you the environmental implications and what degree of remediation is needed", the attitude now is one of attempting to answer such questions as:

- What information do we have about the soil, air, water, wildlife, etc.?

- How does that information fit together and what does it really tell us about environmental conditions here?

- Does the area's environmental management framework have integrity, and are regulations and guidelines being applied effectively?

- What is the range of options for environmental protection and remediation?

The environmental audit is being directed by a Steering Committee composed of representatives from the federal, provincial, and municipal governments and the Metropolitan Toronto and Region Conservation Authority, as well as independent environment experts. The Steering Committee organized the audit in two phases. It was thought that, although government files might contain a substantial amount of information, it would not necessarily be complete or comprehensive. Therefore, the task in Phase I was to collect and analyse existing information; describe environmental legislation, standards, regulations, and guidelines affecting the area; and identify gaps. No new tests of soil, water or air were undertaken in that part of the Committee's work, but testing will be included in Phase II.

The Steering Committee also recognized that private landowners and tenants in the area would probably have useful information on past and present uses of sites, testing of soils and groundwater, etc. Therefore, letters were sent to all identified occupants in the area, asking them for their co–operation and help. The response was encouraging and information continues to be offered and added to the database.

By the time Phase II is completed, the Royal Commission should be able to describe the nature, distribution, and severity of pollution problems, as well as the ecological and recreational values associated with the environment of the designated area. Environmental issues and opportunities will be identified to provide a basis for developing options for environmental protection and remediation.

We define an ecosystem approach as one that takes into account air, land, water, and living organisms, including humans, and the interactions among them. We applied the concept to the first phase of the audit and will develop it further in the second. (A fuller description is provided in Chapter 7.)

As a first step in the audit, the Committee set up a study team consisting of five work groups to collect information on: water, air, soils and groundwater, natural heritage, and the built heritage. (Their reports will be published by the Royal Commission as technical papers.) Information was assessed under three categories — the "terrestrial environment", the "aquatic environment", and the "atmospheric environment" — so that links between the various elements could be developed.

The terrestrial environment (Chapter 2) includes soils and groundwater, terrestrial wildlife, the built heritage, and human occupation of the area. The aquatic environment (Chapter 3) is defined as the Don River watershed, a lake–water envelope around the audit area, the Outer Harbour, and the water bodies within the area (Keating Channel, Ship Channel, and the Turning Basin), as well as the aquatic wildlife and human use of these bodies of water. The atmospheric environment (Chapter 4) includes the air–envelope surrounding Toronto; the climate that governs the area; and internal sources of noise and air pollution.

Chapter 5 is a review of the roles and responsibilities of various stakeholders, as well as of environmental legislation, regulations, and guidelines that govern environmental conditions in the area. Chapter 6 discusses the gaps in information identified in this first phase, and includes some options for Phase II research. Finally, Chapter 7 offers a preliminary synthesis of the three environments and a description of the ecosystem they comprise.

The Steering Committee and the work groups have been conscious that the audit is not being undertaken in a vacuum: related studies are going on at different levels of government and as part of various government programs; moreover, private–sector initiatives affect the environment of the area in both the short and long term.

The Steering Committee and work groups recognize the need to relate the analysis, conclusions, and recommendations in the audit to the work done elsewhere, while avoiding duplication. This effort started in Phase I and will continue in Phase II; it will include, but not be limited to, work carried out by:

- the IJC, in regard to water quality and water level issues in the Great Lakes;

- the consultation process Environment Canada is implementing in formulating its Green Plan environmental agenda;

- the federal–provincial Metro Toronto Remedial Action Plan (RAP);

- the Province of Ontario's Municipal Industrial Strategy for Abatement (MISA) and its promotion of Guidelines for the Decommissioning and Clean–up of Sites in Ontario;

- Metropolitan Toronto's plans for upgrading the Main Sewage Treatment Plant;

- THC's application of Open Water Guidelines for Lakefill and its Guidelines for Decommissioning and Clean–up ; and

- the City of Toronto's Lower Don Valley Task Force, and the environmental studies being undertaken by the City as part of the planning process for the Ataratiri housing project.

Like other aspects of the Royal Commission's work, the audit has been developed and organized to encourage maximum public consultation. Community representatives and independent environmental experts are members of the Steering Committee and work groups, and the reports of both phases will be subject to public hearings before the Royal Commission reaches any conclusions and submits its recommendations to government.

Therefore, members of the public are invited to participate in the Royal Commission's hearings on the results of the first phase of the audit and on options for the Phase II work program. As noted earlier, these hearings on waterfront environment and health issues resume at the Commission's Toronto offices on 22 May 1990.

1. HISTORICAL BACKGROUND

The history of a place can tell us about our past, what shapes the present, and what forces may influence the future. The East Bayfront/Port Industrial Area has a dramatic history, in which water was transformed into land in order to create a port and an industrial land base. We found that both the built and the natural heritage were important influences in the area and we are convinced that maintaining continuity with the past will be important as redevelopment occurs.

NATIVE PRESENCE

Archaeological studies of the Toronto region suggest that most native villages were concentrated on rivers, usually at least a kilometre from Lake Ontario. Such areas provided a combination of features that were suitable for permanent habitation: fresh water, tillable soil, proximity to mixed hunting areas, and elevated defensible positions. The shores and wetlands along the lake were used for hunting and fishing, with temporary camps providing a base during the appropriate seasons. No archaeological evidence of native presence in the Toronto waterfront area has been found, presumably because the short duration of visits to the lakeshore did not lead to the accumulation of materials.

The peninsula enclosing the waters and wetlands of Toronto Bay would probably have been a favoured location for native camps, because of the variety and productivity of wildlife in this area. Elizabeth Simcoe, whose husband was the Lieutenant–Governor of Upper Canada from 1792 to 1796, kept a detailed diary of life in the area; she observed that the Indians came here to recuperate from illness, taking refuge under the shady trees and bathing in the cool lagoons.

EUROPEAN SETTLEMENT

When Europeans first arrived in the area in the late 18th century, they were attracted by the sheltered waters of Toronto Bay, protected to the south by the curving sandy

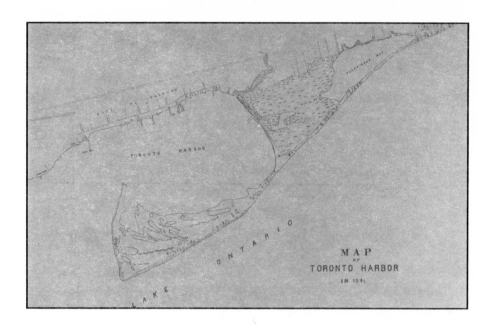

Map of the Toronto Harbour Area in 1841.

Courtesy of City of Toronto Archives (CRC# MT00508L1)

The wetlands of Ashbirdge's Bay in 1904

Courtesy of City of Toronto Archives (DPW 14– Vol. 4, #69).

peninsula later known as Fisherman's Island. The Don River emptied into the eastern end of Toronto Bay, forming a 486–hectare (1,200–acre) delta marsh in Ashbridge's Bay.

Toronto Bay was, and still is, largely open water, whereas Ashbridge's Bay was composed of ponds, weedy lagoons, bogs, and small islands, bounded by Fisherman's Island. Early naturalists, including Mrs. Simcoe, Ernest Thompson–Seton, J.H. Fleming, and others, found Ashbridge's Bay a paradise for wildlife. They wrote about great flocks of passenger pigeons, ducks that rose from the water in such numbers that they made "a noise like thunder", thousands of snow buntings, wolves feeding on deer, and many sightings of rare birds. Pond lilies, marsh marigolds, arrowhead, cane grass, and duckweed grew in abundance.

In 1793, the Ashbridge family built a log house on the east bank of the Don River near its outflow to the Bay. Later, cottages and summer homes were constructed on the peninsula and adjacent islands. Hunting, fishing, and trapping were both a way of life and major commercial activities, based on the large populations of muskrats, turtles, fish, ducks, and shorebirds.

LANDSCAPE CHANGE DURING THE 19TH CENTURY

The Don River created several problems for the developing town of Toronto. Its meanderings as it approached the lake interfered with infrastructure, such as railway tracks. In 1887, work was begun to straighten the course of the lower Don River and reclaim a low swampy area in the floodplain for use by the railways.

In 1834, Hugh Richardson, the first Harbour Master, complained about the impact of the river on the harbour:

> From the moment the peninsula raised its protecting head above the waters, and screened the Don from the surges of the lake, the Don, like a monster of

ingratitude, has displayed such destructive industry as to displace by its alluvial disgorgings by far the greater part of the body of water originally enclosed by the peninsula.

The river's alluvial disgorgings created a need for expensive dredging to remove silt and maintain the harbour at a depth adequate for navigation. Various schemes were proposed, to divert the Don from flowing into the harbour and confine sediment deposition to Ashbridge's Bay. In 1870, the Harbour Trust constructed a breakwater along the south side of the mouth of the Don, designed to reduce siltation, improve navigation, and reclaim some land south of the breakwater. However, the engineers had overestimated their ability to manage natural processes: in 1875 the channel was so shallow that a number of ships went aground and, by 1886, successive spring floods had destroyed the breakwater.

Several major storms in the 1850s had breached Fisherman's Island, creating the Eastern Gap and separating the Toronto Islands from the peninsula, which caused erosion problems along the shoreline. In response to this situation, as well as because of the need to improve navigability, a new breakwater was constructed across the eastern end of the harbour, separating it from Ashbridge's Bay. While this "government breakwater" was effective in reducing the amount of debris, silt, and other matter being deposited into the harbour, which was disrupting shipping, it also reduced water circulation in Ashbridge's Bay.

The marshlands and the deeper waters of Ashbridge's Bay had already been polluted by city sewers and by the discharge from Gooderham and Worts's cattle byres, comprising wastes from as many as 4,000 animals. Once the breakwater was created, water stagnated and pollution became a serious health hazard. People became concerned about the condition of the bay, which one local newspaper described as a "malarial swamp...teeming with pestilence and disease". In an attempt

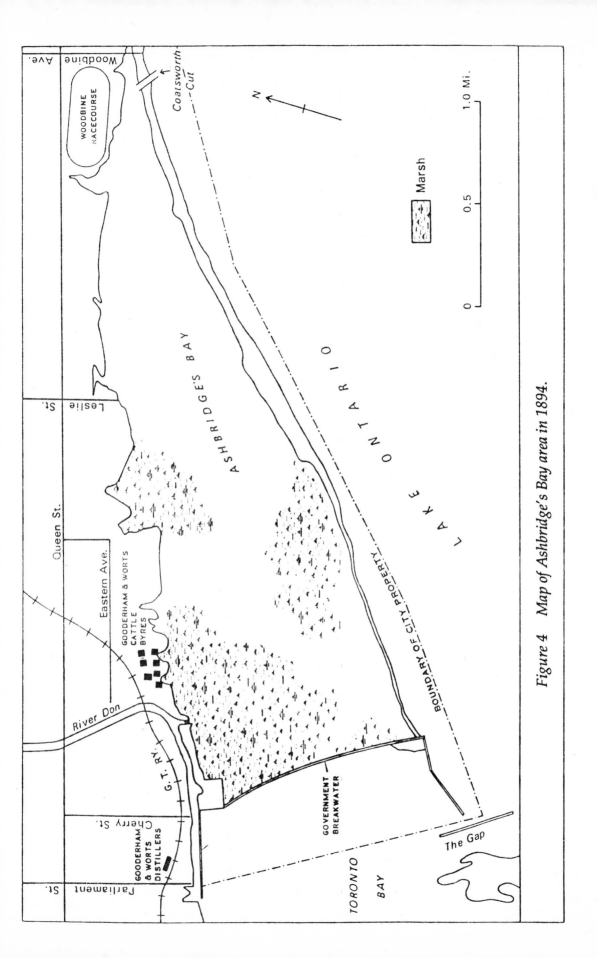

Figure 4   Map of Ashbridge's Bay area in 1894.

to improve circulation and water quality, an opening to the lake, Coatsworth Cut, was created at the eastern end of the peninsula.

THE 20TH CENTURY: CONSTRUCTION OF THE LANDSCAPE

By the beginning of the 20th century, Toronto's harbour was the object of considerable derision: it was inadequate for navigation, its water was polluted, access was obstructed by up to eight sets of railway tracks, and control of waterfront development was highly suspect.

After years of dispute between the City and the Harbour Trust about land ownership, control of development, and financing of proposed harbour improvements, the Board of Toronto Harbour Commissioners (THC) was established in 1911 and paved the way for co–ordinated, sweeping changes to the waterfront. Within eight months after it came into existence, the THC had developed a comprehensive waterfront plan, with development at the eastern end of the harbour a priority. The area was to have an industrial zone, lots for summer homes, and a major park along its southern edge.

Over the next two decades, implementation of the 1912 plan proceeded rapidly: construction of retaining walls was begun in 1913, and, in 1914, lakefilling began at Ashbridge's Bay, using the "Cyclone", the largest and most powerful floating dredge on the continent. By 1922, approximately 200 hectares (500 acres) of land had been created, and, by 1936, the framework of the retaining walls was finally completed. The mouth of the Don River was reconfigured, creating a 90–degree turn into the Keating Channel. A 122–metre (400–foot) wide shipping channel and turning basin were constructed.

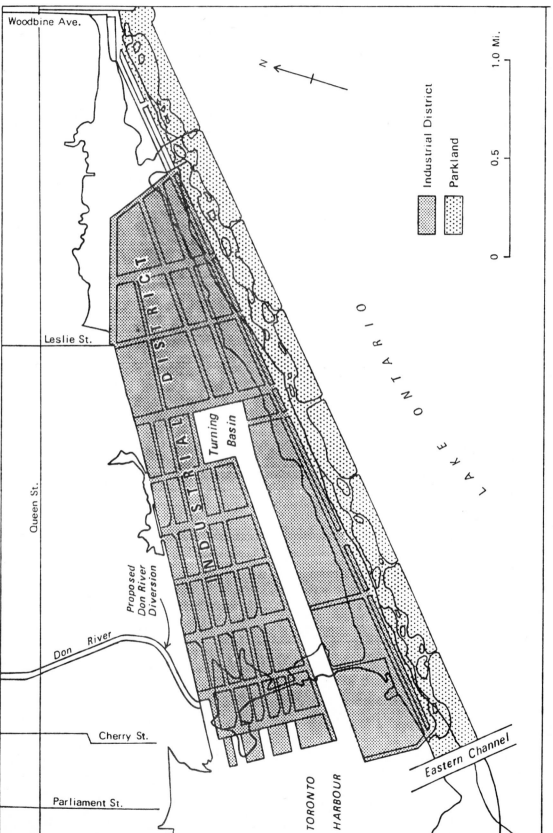

Figure 5   *Toronto Harbour Commissioners Plan for Eastern Section of Toronto's Waterfront, 1912.*

In addition to dredgeate from the bottom of the lake, material from construction activities was used to fill in the bay. For example, in 1914 alone, approximately 46,000 cu³ (60,000 cubic yards) of fill consisting of excavation material and brick rubble were deposited at a site south of the original foot of Cherry Street. Over the next few decades, the Port District provided a convenient dumping ground for a variety of materials, including construction debris, excavated soil from subway development, asphalt, sewage sludge, incinerator ash, and municipal refuse.

A network of roads and railways was developed to provide links with the Port. In 1918, a bascule bridge (lift–bridge) was constructed on Cherry Street, over the Keating Channel; it was replaced in 1968 by a new bridge. The bascule bridge over the Ship Channel, opened to traffic in 1931, is still in operation.

As land was created and serviced, a variety of industries moved in, the first, in 1917, being British Forgings Limited, which processed scrap steel into artillery for the war effort. By 1931, some 41 firms had located in the Port Industrial Area, including oil refineries, oil tank storage farms, coal storage yards, coal tar distillation plants, tanneries, lumber yards, and metal foundries.

Development of the East Bayfront between Yonge and Parliament streets was held up by years of complicated negotiations involving the City, the THC, and the railways. Finally, in 1924, an agreement was reached to allow construction of a railway viaduct on reclaimed land created from fill dredged from Toronto Bay. Nine underpasses beneath the viaduct provided improved access to the East Bayfront and the Port Industrial Area.

However, development of the East Bayfront area was further postponed until the 1950s, when the opening of the St. Lawrence Seaway created expectations of increased ship traffic in the Port of Toronto. A dockwall was constructed, and lakefilling behind it provided a land base for three marine terminals (MT 27, 28, and 29). A sugar refinery (formerly Canada and Dominion Sugar Company Ltd, now Redpath Sugar Ltd.) was the first industry to locate there as a direct result of the new seaway.

The summer homes and grand waterfront park proposed for the southern edge of the Port Industrial District in the 1912 plan never materialized. However, reclaimed land not immediately used for buildings, docks or storage areas was soon colonized by weedy plants, shrubs, willows, and other flora, providing habitat for numerous species of birds, especially during migration.

In the 1940s, a large marsh still remained in the area between Leslie Street and Coatsworth Cut, providing diverse wildlife habitats, as well as stands of cattails, waterholes, and muddy flats, which supported a bounty of waterfowl, shorebirds, and other wildlife. Adjacent to Coatsworth Cut was a small wilderness of shrubs and small trees, known to local naturalists as the Jungle, a habitat for many land birds such as cuckoos, flycatchers, vireos, warblers, finches, and sparrows. In 1952, the Jungle and the last remaining vestige of the Ashbridge's Bay marsh were both destroyed to make way for the Main Sewage Treatment Plant.

Even before the THC plan of 1912 — in the early years of the 19th century — business people in the Town of York and its successor, the City of Toronto, had been urging that an outer harbour be built to expand the Port of Toronto. Later ideas for an outer harbour envisaged creating a new area for port development and providing facilities to relocate shipping activities from the Inner Harbour. That, in turn, would free up land in the eastern waterfront for redevelopment to commercial and residential uses.

Some preparatory filling was undertaken along the southern shore of the Port District during the 1950s and construction of a protective breakwater was begun at the foot of Leslie Street in the 1960s. However, a second harbour was never needed, and the Outer Harbour Headland, more popularly known as the Leslie Street Spit, has developed through natural processes into a rich wilderness for wildlife with an astonishing variety of plant and animal species.

The THC's most recent land creation project in the study area is the Outer Harbour Marina, which was begun in 1986. It includes a Marina Breakwater, intended to provide 1,200 mooring slips, and a Marina Centre at the base of the breakwater. The Marina Centre will include commercial activities, light marine–related industries, and recreational activities.

Several issues have arisen in connection with the Outer Harbour Marina project: the environmental impact of lakefilling, traffic conflicts among recreational users of the Outer Harbour, and the impact on wildlife at the Leslie Street Spit. In addition, bulldozing at the base of the marina during construction destroyed field and shrub communities and wet depressions that had provided valuable wildlife habitats.

SUMMARY

The reshaping of Toronto's Central Waterfront was an impressive accomplishment. The Toronto Harbour Commissioners' 1912 plan guided construction of more than 526 hectares (1,300 acres) of land in its eastern part. These landscape changes allowed shipping and industrial activities to be established, but they have been accompanied by dramatic changes in the environment. The wetlands of Ashbridge's Bay, once a wildlife paradise and renowned hunting ground, have vanished. The remaining natural heritage — the plants and animals that live in and migrate through the area — is testimony to the persistence of many species of wildlife despite dramatic habitat change. At the same time, the area's built heritage is a reminder of the power humans have to shape a port and industrial centre.

The East Bayfront/Port Industrial Area is once again about to change. The environmental questions raised by yet another shift lead to the need for an environmental audit. The next three chapters examine the existing terrestrial, aquatic, and atmospheric environments in order to gain a preliminary understanding of the problems and opportunities they could present for the future.

2. THE TERRESTRIAL ENVIRONMENT

In the East Bayfront/Port Industrial Area, the terrestrial environment has been shaped by dramatic changes in the landform over the last century. Where recycling industries, food processing plants, and petroleum storage tanks stand today, a hundred years ago there was open water, and the wetlands of Ashbridge's Bay were shielded from the lake's waves by the narrow sand spit known as Fisherman's Island.

While some alterations to the natural shores of the harbour began in the 1870s, co–ordinated waterfront development did not begin in earnest until the newly formed THC began work on its 1912 plan to reshape Toronto's waterfront. Because of the extensive lakefilling carried out by the THC in the wake of its 1912 plan, little or nothing remains of the original Fisherman's Island. Virtually all of the lands from Yonge Street to Coatsworth Cut (now known also as Ashbridge's Bay) and south of Lakeshore Boulevard have been constructed since 1912. In some 40 years of activity, the East Bayfront/Port Industrial Area has been formed because breakwalls were built, massive hydraulic dredging of sand from the Inner Harbour and the lake was undertaken, and the area has been filled with construction rubble and other solid wastes.

The most visible parts of the terrestrial environment are the structures and buildings associated with the port and industrial activities, as well as the vegetation and wildlife along the north shore of the Outer Harbour and in vacant lots. What is not visible is the degradation of soils and groundwater caused by decades of industrial activity. This chapter reviews existing information on three aspects of the terrestrial environment: the built landscape, soils and groundwater, and terrestrial wildlife.

THE BUILT LANDSCAPE

The landform of the East Bayfront/Port Industrial Area, based on a well–defined framework of dockwalls, slips, and ship channels, was created as an important part of Toronto's

The Port Industrial Lands. A heritage of docks and channels, ships and barges, silos, stacks and storage tanks. The entire area was created by lakefilling. A variety of port and industrial uses are evident: docking, trucking, storage, refining, recycling etc. The Cherry Beach/North Shore area to the right of the photo is comparatively natural.

Courtesy of Metro Toronto and Region Conservation Authority.

economic history. The area has been (and still is) used for a variety of port and industrial activities: shipping, transfer and storage of materials, energy generation, sewage treatment, refining, processing, and manufacturing. The pattern of roads, bridges, railways, and docks in the area reflects the needs of many companies engaged in these activities for transfers between and amongst different modes of transport.

Ship channels and docks penetrate the area; as a result, barges, ships, dredges, tugs, and freighters are juxtaposed with the built landscape. The protected waters of the Outer Harbour are used by boardsailors and small boats.

The scale of the built landscape is large, dominated by silos, warehouses, factories, tall stacks, bulk fuel storage tanks, and the like. Major roads like Commissioners and Cherry streets were built as wide boulevards and planted with avenues of street trees. On a smaller scale, features such as train buffers, bollards, satellite dishes, and piles of stored materials provide more detailed clues to the area's transportation, communications, and industrial activities.

Architectural styles in the designated area's industrial buildings are generally utilitarian. While a detailed heritage assessment of the area is currently being undertaken by the THC, the architectural qualities of one 1920 building, the former branch of the Bank of Montreal at 309 Cherry Street, have already caused it to be listed in the City of Toronto's Inventory of Heritage Properties.

SOILS AND GROUNDWATER

The characterization of the soil and groundwater conditions of the East Bayfront/Port Industrial Area started with an understanding of the human processes that have shaped the area, based on an inventory of historical and existing land uses. Existing information on soils and groundwater was reviewed, including recent geotechnical and decommissioning studies undertaken for sites on which redevelopment is planned.

The geotechnical reports provided information on soil types and layers, soil strength, groundwater conditions, and general subsurface characteristics of importance for building foundations and the placement of roads and utilities. The decommissioning reports contributed data on upper soil layers, focussing on the chemical content of soils and/or groundwater.

Soil Types

Like all marshlands, the original wetlands at the mouth of the Don River were varied: in some places, there was open water, in others islands of emergent vegetation such as cattails. The thickness of fill in the area is therefore not uniform. Despite the variation, the soils and bedrock can be characterized in terms of six layers, the top two of which are of most importance for the purposes of this study.

The upper layer consists of heterogeneous fill including excavated materials, construction rubble, asphalt, sludge, and ash; it is commonly between 0.5 and 2.5 metres (1.6 to eight feet) in depth except in parts of the southeastern section of the study area where it sometimes reaches almost eight metres (26 feet) in thickness.

Below the upper layer is a stratum created by hydraulic dredging of sediments from the harbour and lake. It consists largely of silty and sandy material, and ranges in depth from 0.6 metres (two feet) to eight metres (26 feet).

Underneath the layers of fill and dredgeate are the original upper lakebed sediments from the bottom of the marsh — although, in some cases, these were disturbed during the lakefilling operation and the boundary between the layers may not be well defined. These original sediments consist of peat and organically rich silts and clays.

The next stratum is composed of lower lakebed sediments that are largely fine- to medium-grained sand, with small deposits of materials such as clay, silt, coarse sand and gravel, and boulders. Below the lower lakebed sediments lies a thin stratum of till and/or weathered bedrock, composed of clayey silts, sand, and shale fragments. The bottom bedrock layer is weathered shale of the Georgian Bay Formation. This is found at depths ranging from 14 to 24 metres (46 to 79 feet) below the surface of the ground.

The Possible Impact of Past and Current Industrial Uses

Precise characterization of soil and groundwater conditions in the study area can be obtained only through a program of sampling and analysis of soil and groundwater at each site. However, predictions about the likelihood of contamination can be made by reviewing past and current industrial uses. A thorough inventory of historical land uses in the study area was conducted by examining THC condition plans, the City of Toronto's fire insurance plans, Metropolitan Toronto city directories, and other relevant sources dating back as far as 1900.

This inventory identified 123 sites in the area, and provided a chronology of industrial land uses with historical site plans. Many of these sites were found to have had similar former land uses, such as petroleum or coal storage, activities that, historically, depended on the proximity of water, road, and rail transportation routes. An analysis of industrial activity over time shows that the sites can be grouped into eleven major industrial sectors; they can be found in Table 1, where the likelihood of residual contamination of soil and groundwater from each sector is also indicated. (In many cases, a site was used for a variety of industrial activities over the years.)

TABLE 1: SUMMARY OF FORMER LAND USES

Industrial Activity	Number Of Sites With Similar Former Land Uses	Likely (1) Residual Contamination
Petroleum Product Storage, Refining, and Distribution	38	Yes
Coal Storage and Distribution	39	Maybe
Primary Metal Industries and Fabricated Metal Products	23	Yes
Offices and Retail/Wholesale Outlets	16	No
Docking and Trucking Facilities	14	No
Food Processing, Storage, and Distribution	10	No
Chemical and Building Material Storage and Distribution	10	Maybe
Metals Recycling	10	Yes
Vacant Land and Parkland	10	No
Tar Distillation and Briquetting Plants	5	Yes
Miscellaneous (2)	30	Maybe

(1) Contamination of soil and groundwater may also result from materials used for lakefilling and from migration of polluted groundwater, even in those areas where residual contamination from industry is not expected.

(2) Includes: incinerator; commercial refrigeration equipment; aggregate and cement industries; paper and allied products; wood industries; glass and plastic industry; hydro substations; sewage treatment plant; works yards; and RCAF storage.

Of the 123 sites in the study area, 38 were or are used for the refining, storage or distribution of petroleum products. Available information suggests that such land use typically results in contamination of soil and groundwater with petroleum products, due to spillage and leakage. In addition to the potential presence of free product (oil or gasoline), such sites will often be contaminated with volatile organics (such as benzene, toluene, and xylene), phenols, and polycyclic aromatic hydrocarbons (PAHs).

Thirty–nine sites were used for coal storage and distribution. Such land use may result in slightly elevated levels of some heavy metals and PAHs in soils, and high levels of sulphate and low pH in groundwater.

Twenty–three sites in the area were used for primary metals industries and the fabrication of metal products. The soil and groundwater at such sites may contain elevated levels of heavy metals, oil and grease, volatile organics, and PAHs.

Metal recycling operations were carried out at ten sites, where elevated levels of iron, aluminum, and other heavy metals may be resident in the soil.

Storage of chemicals and building materials occurred at ten sites in the area. Depending on the nature of the materials stored, some residual soil and groundwater contamination may be present.

Five sites were formerly used for tar distillation and briquetting plants. At such sites, elevated levels of volatile organics, phenols, and PAHs may be remnant in both soil and groundwater. Coal tar as free product may also be present.

Miscellaneous industrial activities ranging from cement industries to glass manufacturing were identified at 30 sites in the area. Depending on the nature of the industrial activity, a degree of contamination of soil and groundwater may be present at some sites. In particular, hydro substations may be a source of PCB contamination of soil, and disposal of ash from public utilities may have left residual contaminants.

Industrial activities that are not expected to have contributed to significant contamination of soil and groundwater include: office and retail outlets; food processing, storage, and distribution; docking and trucking activities; vacant land; and parkland. The majority of sites in the East Bayfront area have only been used for office buildings, retail or wholesale outlets, or warehouse space. The soils and groundwater in this area are therefore less likely to have been affected by land uses than those in the Port Industrial Area, which is dominated by "dirtier" industrial uses.

Nevertheless, it is possible that even at sites that have not been occupied by polluting industries, contaminants may be present from other sources. For example, in creating the land by lakefilling, a variety of materials was placed over dredged sediments throughout the study area. They included municipal trash, construction rubble, and excavated material, and may be a source of metal contamination at some sites. Soils in the vicinity of the Gardiner/Lakeshore transportation corridor may have elevated levels of lead resulting from vehicle emissions. Migration of groundwater from contaminated sites may pollute adjacent ones.

Soil Conditions

Information on soil quality in the study area is limited, and was available during Phase 1 of the environmental audit for only 12 of the 123 sites. Seven of these were (or are) used for refining, storing or distributing petroleum products. The remainder include two sites on which coal tar products were distilled or stored, an iron foundry (on two sites), and one site that had been vacant. In most cases, soil studies were carried out in the framework established by the Ontario Ministry of the Environment's (MOE's) 1989 *Guidelines on the Decommissioning and Clean–up of Sites in Ontario*.

These guidelines may come into effect when a change in land use is proposed for an industrial site. Although not legally enforceable, they have been used to require clean–up or remediation of a site when certain criteria are exceeded. These include conductivity, pH, and levels of oil and grease and selected metals. At this time, MOE does not have criteria for specific organic contaminants. The guidelines specify levels of clean–up for two broad groupings of land uses: acceptable levels of contamination for agricultural, residential, and park uses are slightly lower than those acceptable for commercial and industrial uses.

The soil tests undertaken for the 12 studies reviewed often used only those criteria covered by the MOE guidelines. In some cases, however, testing included evaluation of additional factors such as volatile organics (benzene, toluene, and xylene), polycyclic aromatic hydrocarbons (PAHs), and polychlorinated biphenyls (PCBs).

Soil contamination was extensive in the seven sites at which petroleum products were or are being refined, stored or distributed: the ground surface was often found to contain patches of oily products, particularly in areas where petroleum products were loaded or transferred. Oil and grease analysis of soils below the surface gave general indications of site contamination by petroleum products. Where analysed, samples for oil and grease exceeded the provincial clean–up guidelines in anywhere from 16 to 60 per cent of the samples.

Levels of organic vapour concentrations, which were measured at five of the sites, ranged from low to high levels that indicate an explosion hazard. Analyses for PAHs found them at two sites, the highest levels being noted in soils with the highest oil and grease concentrations. Levels of metals at the seven sites varied, but at each location, at least one metal exceeded the MOE clean–up guidelines.

As previously mentioned, soil studies were reviewed for five sites used for purposes other than petroleum refining, storage, and distribution. At both the sites once occupied by a foundry, levels of oil and grease, cadmium, and lead exceeded provincial clean–up guidelines. High levels of mercury were found at one site and high levels of PAHs at the other. At the two sites where coal tar products were once distilled or stored, mercury, oil, and grease exceeded provincial clean–up guidelines, and high levels of PAHs were found.

At the site of proposed development at Unwin Avenue and Leslie Street, which has been vacant for most of the time, potentially explosive levels of methane gas were found in some boreholes. Levels of resistivity, sulphate, and chloride in some boreholes were found to be high enough to adversely affect normal portland cement or steel building piles. Levels of lead, copper, and zinc exceeding provincial clean–up guidelines were found, as well as slightly elevated levels of cadmium. The amounts of heavy metals were attributed to construction debris and ash that have been deposited on the site.

When contamination was identified at a site, it was found to vary significantly across that site.

Physical Characteristics of the Groundwater

The land in the study area is low, and the water table is generally only 0.4 to two metres (1.3 to 6.6 feet) below grade. The general tendency of the groundwater is to flow from the highest points of land to the lowest and, ultimately, to surface waters (the Keating and Ship channels, Lake Ontario, and the harbours). Locally, however, groundwater flows can be influenced by buried features like pipelines and watermains that are usually surrounded by granular fill, and thus act as drains for groundwater. Calculations showed that the rate of groundwater flow can vary from 0.02 to 90 metres (less than an inch to almost 300 feet) a year.

Groundwater Quality

The study team reviewed eight studies of groundwater quality that had been undertaken as part of the industrial decommissioning process. Six of the sites are or were used for petroleum refining, storage, and distribution; the remaining two were once used for coal tar distillation and storage.

The provincial guidelines for decommissioning industrial sites do not address groundwater quality. Instead, groundwater quality is usually compared to the Provincial Drinking Water Objectives. Because the groundwater in the study area is not used as a source for drinking water, it may be more appropriate to use the Provincial Water Quality Objectives (PWQO), which address the impact of water on aquatic habitat and recreational uses. The PWQO contain acceptable concentrations for phenols, some volatile organic compounds, PCBs, and some heavy metals.

Petroleum products are immiscible in water and, while a small amount may dissolve, they remain essentially as a separate phase (or "free product") that usually sits on top of the groundwater. At each of the four petroleum product sites where it was measured, such free product ranged from a thin film to 1.1 metres (3.6 feet) in thickness.

Phenols were found to be ubiquitous at all eight sites, and levels at each exceeded the PWQO. Benzene, toluene, and xylene are the lighter, volatile fractions of petroleum products, and were analysed at five sites. At these, levels of at least one and, in some cases, all three, compounds were found to exceed PWQO. PCBs were found in excess of PWQO in the groundwater at one of two sites where sampling was undertaken. PAHs (which are not covered under the PWQO) were found at the one site where testing was carried out for these compounds.

Analysis of metals in groundwater was carried out at five sites, and PWQO were exceeded for at least one metal at each. The levels of metals varied throughout the study area and, in part, this may reflect contamination from the material used for landfilling prior to the establishment of industries in the area.

TERRESTRIAL WILDLIFE

Although most of the original wildlife habitats of Ashbridge's Bay have been destroyed, there are still some semi–natural areas that support a surprising variety of resident and migrating species. Although there are few recent published studies on terrestrial wildlife in the area, records and notes contributed to the study team by naturalists provided comprehensive information about some forms of wildlife, particularly birds and butterflies.

Figure 6 illustrates the key areas of wildlife habitat, which are concentrated along the north shore of the Outer Harbour, at the Base of the Leslie Street Spit, and in vacant lots in the industrial area[1].

Vegetation

Vacant lots, unmaintained roadsides, the extensive areas south of Unwin Avenue between the Eastern Gap and Leslie Street, and the base of the Leslie Street Spit support naturally seeded field and shrub communities. The open fields include many species of grasses and wildflowers, such as aster, dock, goatsbeard, goldenrod, ladies' tresses, milkweed, mullein, sedge, and sweet white clover. Shrubby areas include willow, sumach, and dogwood.

Young groves of trees, such as cottonwoods and willows, are developing in field and shrub areas where natural succession has been occurring for some time. Mature woodland, consisting of eastern cottonwood and black willow, occurs in the Cherry Beach area[2]. Much of the shrub understorey, predominantly red osier dogwood and honey-suckle, has been cleared and replaced with mown grass.

---

[1] Figure also shows areas where wintering waterfowl concentrate, including lagoons in the Metro Toronto Sewage Treatment Plant; these aquatic species are discussed in Chapter 3.

[2] Cherry Beach refers to the public beach and recreation area at the western end of the north shore of the Outer Harbour. This area has had several names over the years. In 1935, it was called Simcoe Park but from 1940 to 1945 it was Clark Beach. The best-known name is Cherry Beach, which was used from 1945 to 1988. In 1988, it was renamed Clark Beach by the City of Toronto.

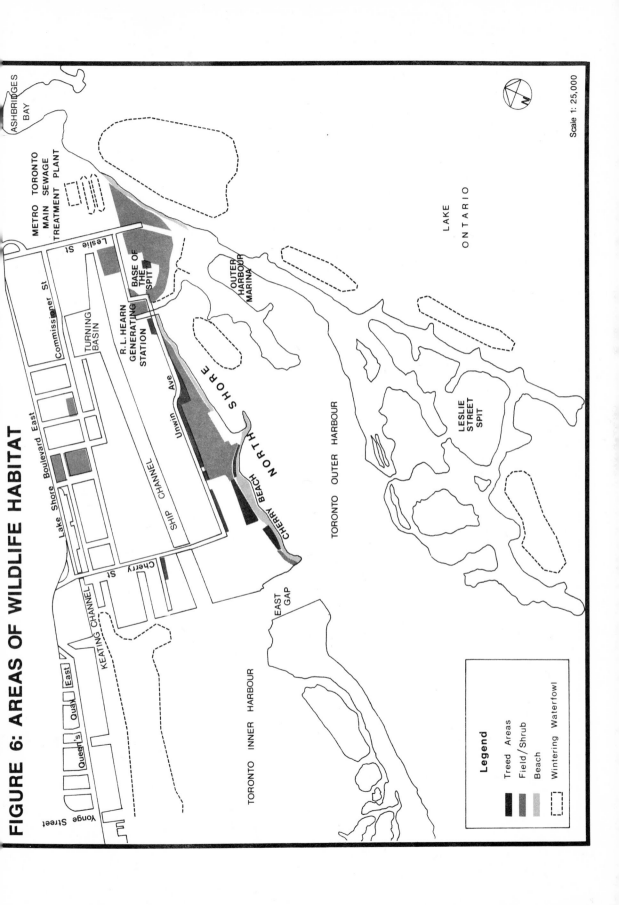

FIGURE 6: AREAS OF WILDLIFE HABITAT

Scale 1: 25,000

ASHBRIDGES BAY

METRO TORONTO MAIN SEWAGE TREATMENT PLANT

Leslie St

Commissioner St

TURNING BASIN

R.L. HEARN GENERATING STATION

BASE OF THE SPIT

OUTER HARBOUR MARINA

Lake Shore Boulevard East

Unwin Ave

SHIP CHANNEL

NORTH SHORE

CHERRY BEACH

KEATING CHANNEL

Cherry St

Queen's Quay East

Yonge Street

EAST GAP

TORONTO INNER HARBOUR

TORONTO OUTER HARBOUR

LESLIE STREET SPIT

LAKE ONTARIO

Legend

■	Treed Areas
▨	Field/Shrub
░	Beach
⌐ ¬	Wintering Waterfowl

Eastern cottonwood is a species found in the Carolinean zone, the northern edge of which lies in Ontario, in the southern and eastern parts of the Great Lakes/St. Lawrence Region. The natural association of eastern cottonwood with a dogwood understorey was once common along the Lake Ontario shoreline but is now comparatively rare. While eastern cottonwoods occur on the Leslie Street Spit and the Toronto Islands, the nearest similar woods are found at Burlington to the west and Presqu'ile to the east.

Patches of wetland vegetation occur in ditches and depressions in vacant lots, along the north shore, and at the base of the spit, particularly in areas adjacent to snow–dumping sites, which are a source of water in spring and sometimes into summer.

The shoreline along the north shore of the Outer Harbour consists of stretches of sand and cobble beach, fringed by associations of shrubs, grasses, and wildflowers.

Invertebrates

The unmanaged vegetation along the north shore, at the base of the spit, in vacant lots, and on roadsides in the designated area provides varied habitat for a wide diversity of invertebrates (butterflies, moths, beetles, ants, bees, wasps, flies, mites, spiders, worms, centipedes, snails, slugs, and many more). In turn, these animals provide food for other wildlife: reptiles, amphibians, birds, and small mammals.

Although there have been no published studies of invertebrates in the area, records of butterflies (27 species) observed by naturalists illustrate the variety of invertebrates supported by the natural vegetation.

Martin Goodman Trail through the North Shore area.
Courtesy of Suzanne Barrett.

Monarch butterfly feeding on nectar of asters.
Courtesy of Verna Higgins.

The relationships between butterflies and their host plants are very specific. For example, the black swallowtail lays eggs on Queen Anne's lace and feeds on the nectar of milkweed flowers. The Acadian hairstreak overwinters and lays eggs on willows; favoured nectar sources are milkweed, white clover, and dogbane. The monarch feeds on nectar from goldenrods and asters, lays eggs on milkweeds, and rests in willows and poplars during migration.

Several butterflies observed in the designated area are migrants, including the red admiral, the painted lady, and the monarch. In general, any natural area along the waterfront is used by migrating butterflies for resting and feeding during migration, as they tend to follow the shoreline, moving from one staging area to the next. In the Toronto region, significant numbers of butterflies congregate during migration on the Toronto Islands, the Leslie Street Spit, and Cherry Beach areas.

The use of the Cherry Beach area by monarch butterflies has a special historical significance: it was there, in the 1950s, that Dr. F.A. Urquhart of the University of Toronto initiated the first monarch tagging program in North America. His research eventually led to the discovery of the monarch's main wintering grounds in Mexico.

Reptiles and Amphibians

Although Ashbridge's Bay Marsh, which must have supported many species of reptiles and amphibians, has been destroyed, the wilder areas along the north shore and at the base of the spit still support a number of species. The seven recorded by naturalists in the 1980s are the American toad, northern leopard frog, common snapping turtle, painted turtle, map turtle, common garter snake, and brown snake.

The key elements of reptile and amphibian habitats in the study area are the temporary ponds, low–lying wet areas, open fields, and sandy beaches. In addition, the snakes spend the winter in a hibernaculum — usually an area of rocks or rubble extending below the frostline. One was known to exist at the base of the spit and was used by common garter snakes. It is not known whether recent bulldozing in this area destroyed the site.

An unusual feature of the garter snake population in the designated area is the occurrence of the uncommon melanistic (dark–coloured) form. This colour morph is rare inland, but also occurs on the Toronto Islands, and the Leslie Street Spit.

Birds

The combination of habitats in the north shore area, at Cherry Beach, the base of the spit, in vacant lots, and at the sewage treatment plant support a great diversity of breeding, migrating, and wintering birds. A total of 260 species was recorded in these areas during the last two decades.

The open field and shrubby areas provide feeding and breeding habitat for such birds as savannah sparrows, horned larks, eastern meadowlarks, killdeer, and bobolinks. Yellow warblers, American goldfinches, song sparrows, northern orioles, and American robins nest in the hedgerows and woods. Red–wing blackbirds and several species of swallow also breed in the area.

As with butterfly migration, birds use natural areas along the waterfront for resting and feeding during migration. The Toronto area is located in the overlapping zones of the two major North American migratory flyways, the Atlantic and the Mississippi. Consequently, the Ashbridge's Bay area has been a traditional staging ground for a great diversity of species that continue to migrate through there, although the habitat has been greatly altered. Different species of birds arrive in succession during fall migration, from mid–July to mid–November, and in the spring, from mid–March to mid–June.

The Leslie Street Spit, extending into Lake Ontario, has a funnelling effect on birds flying north across the lake, because

ATLANTIC FLYWAY

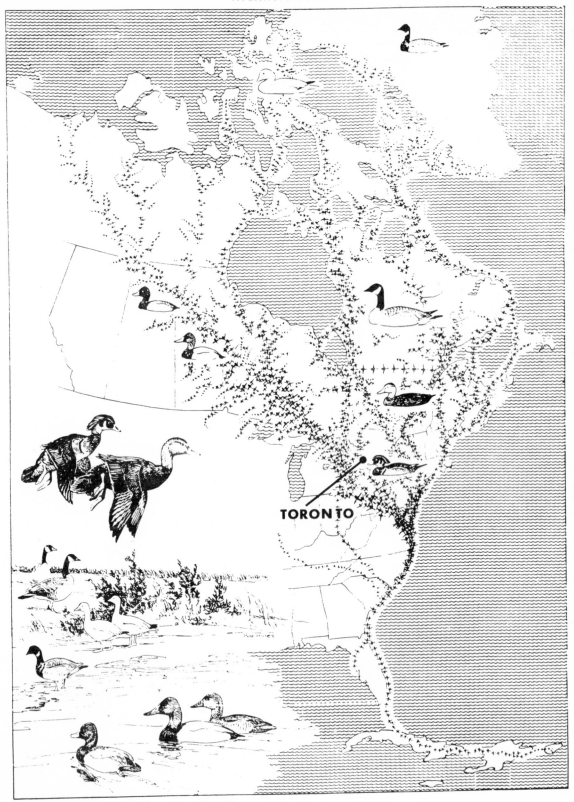

TORONTO

UNITED STATES DEPARTMENT OF THE INTERIOR · FISH AND WILDLIFE SERVICE

MISSISSIPPI FLYWAY

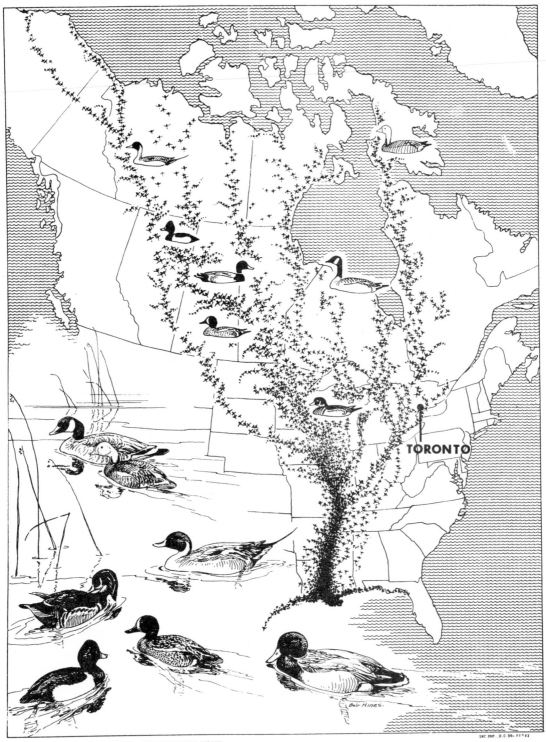

TORONTO

UNITED STATES DEPARTMENT OF THE INTERIOR • FISH AND WILDLIFE SERVICE

it is the first area of land they encounter on the Toronto waterfront. The vegetated areas along the north shore provide a connection to the Don Valley, albeit a fragmented one, for continued migration.

Many birds, such as warblers, waterfowl, shorebirds, sparrows, and blackbirds, migrate in a north–south direction, and depend on shoreline natural areas to provide essential feeding and resting grounds, either before or after the gruelling lake crossing. Other species, including birds of prey such as hawks and eagles, migrate along the shorelines of lakes Ontario and Erie, stopping to feed in open field areas such as the base of the spit.

In the 1950s and '60s, the scrubby tangles amongst the cottonwoods and willows at Cherry Beach were the best place in eastern North America to find saw–whet owls during migration. Because most of the understorey has been removed, the numbers have dwindled, although saw–whet, great horned, long–eared, and barred owls can still be seen in the remaining woods during migration periods.

The close proximity of the north shore, Toronto Islands, and Leslie Street Spit provide complementary habitats for different species throughout the seasons. For example, the north shore area, because it is part of the mainland, is not as exposed to the harsh elements as the spit or the islands. Consequently, the microclimate allows earlier spring and later fall foliage growth, providing greater shelter and food for migrants.

The base of the spit and the north shore are used for loafing or resting by various colonial birds that nest on the Leslie Street Spit. These include ring–billed and herring gulls, black–crowned night herons (a species that is rare in Ontario), caspian terns (rare in Ontario and elsewhere in Canada) and common terns.

Mammals

As for other forms of wildlife, the most important habitat areas for mammals are south of Unwin Avenue, between the Eastern Gap and Coatsworth Cut. Although there are no systematic records of mammals in the designated area, observations made by naturalists indicate that the following mammals are probably resident: bats, eastern cottontail, groundhog, eastern grey squirrel, meadow vole, muskrat, Norway rat, red fox, and raccoon. Occasional sightings of European hare, coyote, beaver, and striped skunk may be of animals just visiting or passing through.

Although there are no records of them, it is likely that other small mammals — shrews, moles, and mice — also occur in the area.

SUMMARY

Our review of the terrestrial environment makes it clear that the East Bayfront/Port Industrial Area encompasses environmental problems and values that are quite typical of old industrial areas. On one hand, soils and groundwater in the area have been contaminated by industrial activities, while, on the other, the built landscape and terrestrial wildlife are reminders of heritage values that should be protected in any future redevelopment of the area.

The built landscape of the East Bayfront/Port Industrial Area recalls an important phase in Toronto's economic history. Assessing the historical significance of this district involves more than simply identifying individual buildings of obvious historical and architectural value. It should encompass the whole environment: the shoreline, landforms, transportation patterns, buildings, and other structures.

Examining the East Bayfront/Port Industrial Area from this broad perspective reveals interesting elements and relationships. The transportation pattern, exemplified by the docks, channels, dockwalls, railway lines, bridges, roads, etc., determined the spatial form of the area. Its economic functions are given physical expression by the factories, stacks, storage tanks, warehouses, and other structures. The ubiquitous presence of ships, boats, and sailing craft illustrates the port functions of the area as well as the recreational values of the waterfront.

Dramatic changes in landscape — the shoreline, landforms, buildings, structures — can create a sense of alienation from the surroundings. By contrast, heritage conservation helps a community retain its direct connection with the people, places, and events of its past and provides a sense of continuity and meaning. However, preserving built heritage does not mean freezing development, nor does it imply that all change is bad. Rather, the challenge is to facilitate beneficial change while preventing the wholesale dislocation that so often accompanies it.

There is evidence that industrial activities in the Port Industrial Area, and to a lesser extent, the East Bayfront, have impaired soil and groundwater conditions. An analysis of previous land uses has allowed the 123 sites in the study area to be grouped into nine industrial sectors. The sites at which soil and groundwater can reasonably be expected to be contaminated include those used for the refining, storage or distribution of petroleum products; primary metal industries; metal recycling; storage of some chemicals; tar distillation and briquetting; and ash disposal associated with public utilities. In addition, contamination may result from materials used in lakefilling, lead in vehicular emissions, and migration of contaminated groundwater across sites.

Data reviewed for specific sites in the study area where testing has been undertaken indicate that soil is degraded, with contamination of portions of all sites exceeding the levels allowed under provincial clean–up criteria for commercial/ industrial use. At most of the sites where groundwater was tested, Provincial Water Quality Objectives (PWQOs) were exceeded for oil and grease, phenols, one or more metals, and volatile hydrocarbons.

The implications are that these sites may require soil remediation before redevelopment for either commercial/industrial use, or for residential/parkland use. The purpose of remediation would be to prevent any adverse impact on human health, vegetation, and aquatic ecosystems. For example, people working or living in the area must be protected from damage caused by direct contact with the soil (e.g., through gardening or children's play); uptake by plants (e.g., vegetables, herbs) grown for consumption; the hazard of explosive vapours; or leakage of contaminants into indoor air.

Some contaminants are toxic to plants, posing potential difficulties for the healthy growth of street trees and other plants used in landscaping. The movement of groundwater to surface waters may carry contaminants to aquatic ecosystems of the channels and harbours and contaminants may be transferred to the atmosphere by volatilization or in dust.

Remediation could be undertaken using *in situ* treatment, or excavation with treatment on or off site. The existing provincial criteria for decommissioning and cleaning up industrial sites do not adequately cover organic contaminants; therefore, if these criteria alone are used for characterization of soil, a less–than–adequate picture of the contaminants at the site will result.

While the abundant wildlife that once flourished in Ashbridge's Bay has disappeared, the area still supports a large variety of wildlife. To a great extent, the value of the area's habitat is the result of benign neglect that has allowed natural processes to maintain woods and field communities, particularly around Cherry Beach, along the north shore of the Outer Harbour, at the base of the spit, and in vacant lots.

One of the most significant values of the study area is as a staging ground during the migration of many species of birds, as well as butterflies, especially the monarch. It also supports many breeding birds, and some mammals, reptiles, and amphibians. The area is strategically located on the waterfront, between the Toronto Islands, Leslie Street Spit, and Don Valley, where its habitat complements theirs and acts as a link for migration and colonization.

The Cherry Beach area has been used as parkland since the land base was created by lakefilling in the 1930s. In conjunction with the north shore area, it is being transferred by the Toronto Harbour Commissioners to the City of Toronto for a city park. Existing natural habitat values suggest that it should be kept in as naturally wild a state as possible.

Improvements to the habitats could also encourage a greater variety of wildlife species. In particular, it would be fitting to re–create wetlands in memory of the Ashbridge's Bay Marsh and to add to the meagre wetlands along the Greater Toronto waterfront, most of which were destroyed during development. They are vital for many kinds of migrating and resident wildlife and should be created wherever the opportunity arises.

© DON PEUTAMAKI

3. *The Aquatic Environment*

In 1793, John Graves Simcoe, the first Lieutenant-Governor of Upper Canada, embarked on his historic project to establish the Town of York, later to become the City of Toronto. At that time and for long after, the fortunes of Toronto were inextricably tied to the water. It was blessed with a natural harbour formed by the Toronto Peninsula (which was later separated by natural forces to become the Toronto Islands and the peninsula that sheltered Ashbridge's Bay). The site offered natural fortification for residents, who would soon be at war with their American neighbours.

The harbour and lake were also good sources of fish for the residents of Muddy York; Ashbridge's Bay, in particular, supplied fish, turtles, and waterfowl for the dinner tables of its inhabitants. At a time when roads were rudimentary at best, transportation by water was vital to commerce. Torontonians lived near the water, used it for commercial trading, feasted on its bounty, and played on it in summer and winter. And people assumed that the lake and the harbour would always absorb the stresses their presence put on them.

The sorry tale of the impact of humans on aquatic ecosystems is written throughout the Great Lakes Basin. Two hundred years of neglect and abuse have wrought an environment that Governor Simcoe would not recognize. Altered shorelines and channelled rivers, polluted waters and contaminated sediments, extirpated fish species and paved wetlands are the legacy of two centuries of European settlement.

In 1985, the International Joint Commission singled out 42 areas in the Great Lakes as highly polluted, and in need of clean-up. The waterfront of Toronto is one such area, designated by the IJC because of bacterial and chemical contamination. The federal and provincial governments are co-ordinating development of a Metropolitan Toronto Remedial Action Plan (RAP) to identify the problems, and to develop remedial action to restore water quality. The RAP is looking at the waterfront from Etobicoke Creek to the Rouge River, and all the watersheds draining the area.

This chapter examines the aquatic environment surrounding the East Bayfront/Port Industrial Area and, based on the research conducted in Phase I of the environmental audit, assesses the condition of the aquatic environment there. It takes an ecosystem approach, dealing with all parts of the aquatic environment: water levels and quality, sediments, and aquatic biota.

WATER LEVELS

Water levels along the Toronto waterfront are governed by the ever-changing level of the Great Lakes. Within any year, these are generally higher in spring and early summer, lower in winter. Although some structures have been built to regulate water levels in the Great Lakes for navigation and power generation purposes, their effects are minimal. Because the study area is low-lying, the potential impact of varying water levels was explored.

A local phenomenon of rapidly rising lake levels known as a "seiche" has been known to occur in Ashbridge's Bay Basin, most recently in 1989. During a violent storm on 14 October 1989, the water level rose by 1.8 metres (5.8 feet) within 20 minutes, and caused extensive damage to boats and docks at the Ashbridge's Bay Yacht Club. No other areas of the harbour are known to be similarly affected by such conditions and, in general, it can be said that high water levels in Lake Ontario do not cause flooding that results in severe damage in the study area.

The Lower Don River and the Keating Channel do not have a history of severe flooding, although there have been occasions when floods have caused property damage. There is the potential for local flooding in the Port Industrial Area if there are ice-jams at various points along the Don River during the run-off season. Yearly dredging of accumulated sediments in the Keating Channel is undertaken to minimize the threat of flooding of areas adjacent to the Don, including that under study.

WATER QUALITY

A number of water quality studies have been undertaken along the Toronto waterfront. Most of them had specific objectives — studying the effects of dredging, for example. Accordingly, the contaminants being analysed, the sampling methods being used, and sites at which sampling was carried out have varied from study to study. Because of inevitable inconsistencies, year-to-year comparisons of data are often difficult.

Water quality objectives or guidelines are the primary tools used by regulatory agencies to determine water quality in terms of human or environmental health. Three official sets of standards exist for water quality: Ontario's Provincial Water Quality Objectives (PWQOs), the federal Canadian Water Quality Guidelines, and the IJC's Water Quality Objectives. They differ in the factors they cover and the levels that are considered "acceptable".

In Phase I of the environmental audit, each factor of ambient water quality conditions was judged according to the most sensitive guideline.

Sources of Pollutants

There are many sources of pollutants in the Toronto waterfront and they include rural run-off from north of Metro's borders, urban stormwater run-off, dry weather seepage, combined sewer overflows, sewage treatment plant effluents, sediments, and atmospheric deposition.

Abatement programs undertaken over the last three decades have resulted in substantial improvements in the water quality of the Don River. Nonetheless, the Don is still the major conduit of pollutants to the Inner Harbour, carrying contaminants from rural and urban run-off, dry weather seepage, and combined sewer overflows.

With the exception of some areas in the north, the Don River watershed is almost totally urbanized. The Don is the receptacle of drainage from some 1,185 storm sewers, 30 combined sewer overflows, several industrial coolant discharges, and the treated municipal effluent from the North Toronto Sewage Treatment Plant. Each year, the Don River discharges into the Inner Harbour about 22,000 tonnes of suspended solids, 54 tonnes of phosphorus, three tonnes of copper, and seven tonnes of lead.

Metro's Main Sewage Treatment Plant receives the sewage generated in a large part of Metro Toronto and, during periods of rain, stormwater contaminated with sewage from combined sewers. Chemicals and metals are dumped into the system from upstream industries and residences. The discharges from the Main Sewage Treatment Plant flow into Ashbridge's Bay and impair water quality in the eastern Toronto waterfront and the eastern shoreline of the study area. During storms, when the flow exceeds the capacity of the plant, partially treated storm water and combined sewage are by-passed into the nearshore of Ashbridge's Bay. The Main Sewage Treatment Plant accounts for significant loadings of phosphorus, copper, zinc, and lead to the waters on the eastern side of the study area.

Sediments can be sources, as well as "sinks", for pollutants including heavy metals and organic chemicals. When disturbed, pollutants in sediments may re-enter the water. During dredging or lakefilling activities, they may be resuspended in the water column, and have a short-term impact on ambient water quality. Contaminants in sediments can also be taken up by benthic (bottom-dwelling) organisms, thus entering the food chain. (See section on "Aquatic Biota" below.)

About 20 storm and combined sewer outfalls discharge directly into the Inner Harbour, a small fraction of the number discharging to the Don River. Combined sewage contains high concentrations of bacteria and metals; while data exist on bacterial loadings from these sources, little is known about the types and levels of metals and organic chemicals they contribute.

Atmospheric deposition is the contribution of chemicals and particulates from the air to the ground and surface waters. It can be wet (rain, snow, hail) or dry (dust) deposition. There is little information available on the amounts and types of contaminants being deposited in the lake and harbour from the air. (The Ministry of the Environment is currently conducting a study to quantify these inputs. See Chapter 4.)

Contaminated groundwater from within the study area is a potential source of pollutants to the waters of the Inner and Outer harbours, and the Keating and Ship channels. (See Chapter 2.)

Spills of fuel from commercial shipping and pleasure boats are another potential, yet largely unquantified, source of pollutants, particularly to the Inner and Outer harbours.

Ambient Water Quality

Eutrophication

Eutrophication in fresh water is generally characterized by excessive growth of aquatic plants because of high levels of nutrients such as phosphorus and nitrogen. If eutrophication is severe, oxygen levels in the water drop and aquatic life cannot be sustained. Phosphorus levels in all waters in the study area exceed the Provincial Objective. Generally, levels of phosphorus and nitrogen are highest near the largest sources of pollution — the Don River and the Main Sewage Treatment Plant.

Since 1969, the average level of phosphorus in the Inner Harbour has decreased significantly, perhaps in part because of reduced loadings from the Don River. However, it may also be attributable to the more general reduction in loadings of

The silt-laden waters of the Don River emptying into the Inner Harbour via the Keating Channel.
Courtesy of the Metropolitan Toronto and Region Conservation Authority.

Cherry Beach is suitable for swimming and board-sailing most of the summer because it is relatively free of bacterial pollution.
Courtesy of Suzanne Barrett

phosphorus from municipalities, which now have regulations that control phosphates in detergents and loadings from sewage treatment plants.

Using a commonly used classification system for eutrophication, the open waters of Lake Ontario can be classified as mesotrophic, or fair. The waters of the Inner Harbour border on a eutrophic state, and the Keating Channel is considered eutrophic, or poor.

Bacteria

The suitability of water for recreational swimming is determined by measuring one particular type of bacteria, fecal coliforms. Levels are used as an indicator of the risk of infection or disease from body contact activities like swimming or boardsailing. In Toronto, signs are posted at beaches where water exceeds the Provincial Objective for fecal coliforms, to warn people of this risk. Most beaches along the Toronto waterfront are "posted" at some time each summer because of high bacterial levels.

Data from the City of Toronto Department of Public Health show that, in terms of bacterial contamination, Cherry Beach, located in the study area in the Outer Harbour, is one of the most consistently clean beaches along the waterfront. In 1988 and 1989, for example, it was not posted at all.

Clarity

The clarity of water is indicated by levels of turbidity and suspended solids. Poor water clarity can have an adverse impact on aquatic life. The greatest influence on turbidity in the study area is the discharge of sediments from the Don River, especially during rainfalls, when turbidity in the Inner Harbour increases to levels well in excess of PWQOs.

Heavy Metals

The waters of the Keating Channel frequently contain concentrations of copper, iron, lead, and zinc that exceed

PWQOs. Levels of copper, iron, lead, and zinc in the Inner Harbour and of copper and iron in the Outer Harbour occasionally exceed the Objectives. The levels in the open waters of Lake Ontario, in contrast, are within the PWQOs for heavy metals. Dredging and lakefilling can elevate metal concentrations in the immediate vicinity of the activity, but it is not known whether they are significant as compared to other factors.

Organic Contaminants

There are few data on levels of organic contaminants in the waters of the study area, and much of the sampling that has been done has been hampered by poor sampling methods. One study carried out in 1983 found that concentrations of polychlorinated biphenyls (PCBs) in Don River effluents and the Inner Harbour well exceeded the objectives set by the International Joint Commission.

SEDIMENTS

Sources

Sediments in the Toronto waterfront are derived mainly from shoreline erosion, discharges from rivers, urban run-off, and lakefilling activities. The natural processes of shoreline erosion, for example, created the Toronto Islands with sand carried from the Scarborough Bluffs.

The major input of sediments to the Inner Harbour is from upstream via the Don River. They originate mainly from urban development and, to a lesser extent, from agricultural activities and streambank erosion. Erosion in the Don watershed peaked between 1950 and 1970 when major urban development was taking place. Since then, because of lower rates of development and better erosion control, erosion rates have dropped to pre-war levels. It is not known whether the recent development boom in York Region has caused a significant increase in sediment loadings to the Don.

As the Don River approaches the waterfront, it makes a sharp 90-degree turn into the Keating Channel, causing much of the sediment load to be deposited in the channel. While yearly dredging is required to avoid upstream flooding, the Keating Channel also acts positively as a trap, stopping sediment from entering the Inner Harbour. The quantity and volume of sediment are important factors in flooding, shipping and navigation, and water clarity. However, the factor that most affects water quality and aquatic life is sediment quality: the level of toxic chemicals bound to sediment particles.

Sediment Quality

The quality of bottom sediments is measured against criteria developed by the Ontario Ministry of the Environment. The Ministry's Open Water Disposal Guidelines are used to determine if dredged material is suitable for disposal in open water. Sediments in which contaminants exceed the guidelines may not be disposed in water, and must be placed in a Confined Disposal Facility. The Open Water Disposal Guidelines cover a number of heavy metals and oil and grease, but have not yet been developed for organic contaminants, except PCBs.

The Ontario Ministry is currently developing more comprehensive Sediment Quality Guidelines for the remediation of contaminated sediments. These will be based on the biological effects on organisms of contaminants in sediments. Once in place, they will make it easier to evaluate the environmental quality of sediments in the study area.

Contamination of bottom sediments in the study area varies somewhat. However, sediments in all the areas — the Keating and Ship channels, the Inner and Outer harbours, and Ashbridge's Bay — exceed the Open Water Disposal Guidelines for at least six pollutants.

As previously mentioned, disturbance of contaminated sediments by dredging or lakefilling has been found to elevate levels of metals in the short term. Even *in situ*, undisturbed sediments that are contaminated can have an effect on aquatic biota.

AQUATIC BIOTA

Benthic Organisms

Benthic organisms live in sediments at the bottom of water bodies. The community structure of benthic organisms is widely used as an indicator of water and sediment quality in fresh water systems. The diversity and type of benthic life reflects the levels of contaminants in the sediment. In highly contaminated areas such as the Keating Channel, there is a low diversity of species, and these tend to be of the pollution-tolerant variety. The number of species increases in deeper, less contaminated open water in and near the study area.

Levels of metals in benthic organisms are relatively similar across the waterfront, in areas considered to be both highly and less polluted. A useful indicator of contaminant uptake by benthic organisms is found by comparing the concentration of a contaminant in an organism with that in the sediment. Such studies show that benthic organisms in the area are not bio-accumulating metals to a significant degree. However, they were found to be bio-accumulating significant levels of some organic compounds — chlordane and hexachlorobenzene in the Keating Channel and Inner Harbour, a metabolite of DDT in the Inner Harbour, and PCBs in Ashbridge's Bay.

Algae and Zooplankton

Despite nutrient-rich conditions throughout the waters bordering on the study area, growth of algae (aquatic plants) is not a nuisance. In areas like the Keating Channel, this is likely due to high levels of turbidity that prevent sunlight from penetrating the water. No recent studies have been done to characterize algal populations in the Toronto Harbour area.

Zooplankton are microscopic animals that are important in the aquatic food chain as consumers of phytoplankton (free-floating algae) and as prey for fish and some sea birds. They typically respond to changes in the aquatic ecosystem through changes in community structure. As with algae, no recent studies have been conducted on zooplankton populations in the Toronto Harbour area. Zooplankton along the Greater Toronto Waterfront are dominated by crustaceans typical of eutrophic conditions.

Fish

Until the early 1800s, the Toronto waterfront and its river mouths and lower reaches teemed with a huge variety and number of fish. Muskellunge, sturgeon, pike, bass, walleye, and American eel were present, as were lake trout and herring. The pressures of development — land-clearing for agriculture and urban expansion, dam construction, waste discharges, and destruction of habitat — caused many species to become rare or extinct.

Most of the desirable, high-quality gamefish have vanished, while the fish that survive in the Toronto Harbour area today are generally the more pollution-tolerant and less valuable species such as carp, yellow perch, and white sucker. Although fish are still found in such places as the Ship Channel, these areas offer very limited natural habitat.

The north shore of the Inner Harbour, because it is concrete-walled and dredged, offers no shallow areas for fish to spawn and feed. The shores and lagoons of the Toronto Islands provide the only good fish habitat in the Inner Harbour. The best habitat remaining in the study area is in the Outer Harbour and Ashbridge's Bay. Sheltered bays created by lakefilling projects have been shown to provide very good habitat for both warm-water and cold-water fish. On the other hand, such constructed habitats are known to contain contaminated sediments.

The issue of contaminants in fish is a complex one. Their biological significance is poorly understood, except for such parameters as PCBs, DDT, and mercury. Factors affecting bio-accumulation are also complex and variable, depending on the host and the particular contaminant. Although regular monitoring of fish for contaminants has been carried out across the Toronto waterfront since 1974, trends in contaminant levels since that time are difficult to confirm. The limited information indicates that levels of PCBs, DDT, and chlordane seem to be decreasing. However, levels of PCBs, in particular, still exceed the International Joint Commission's guidelines for protection of birds and animals.

In the waters of the study area, levels of heavy metals in fish have been studied. The data suggest that no particular location is worse than another in terms of accumulating metals. The highest levels of cadmium, copper, manganese, and mercury were recorded in fish taken from the vicinity of the Leslie Street Spit. The highest levels of lead were found in the Inner Harbour.

The most recent Ministry of the Environment *Guide to Eating Ontario Sports Fish* advises restrictions on eating some sizes of white bass, yellow perch, gizzard shad, northern pike, white sucker, and carp taken from the Outer Harbour and Ashbridge's Bay because of high levels of PCBs, mirex, pesticides, mercury, and, in some cases, other metals.

Aquatic Birds

Some aquatic birds, notably Canada geese and mallard ducks, make their homes year-round on Toronto's shores, but a great variety of others pass through in the spring and fall, or overwinter here. Because of its location on two major migration routes for birds (the Atlantic and Mississippi flyways), the Toronto waterfront has a wide diversity of bird life. (See "Terrestrial Wildlife" in Chapter 2.)

Despite the loss of a great deal of valuable habitat, the study area is still an important stopover during migration for a wide variety of shorebirds. Many species, including dowitchers, yellowlegs, and snipe, could be observed at the base of the spit until bulldozing of low-lying wet depressions was carried out in 1988. A noticeable decrease in species diversity followed this habitat destruction. The lagoons at the sewage treatment plant, however, remain an important habitat for resting and migrating shorebirds. Birds lack a sense of smell, and so rare migrants like godwits, dowitchers, avocets, and Baird's sandpipers can be found at the sewage plant in the spring and fall, along with ardent birdwatchers with handkerchiefs over their noses and binoculars at the ready.

The Toronto area, from Ashbridge's Bay to Humber Bay Park West, is one of three major wintering areas along the northern shore of Lake Ontario for oldsquaw ducks. An Arctic diving duck, the oldsquaw feeds on invertebrates in the sediments of the harbour from November to May, before pairing and then flying north to nest on the shores of Hudson Bay and the Arctic Archipelago. In spite of the contaminated waters of the Keating Channel, it is a prime area for large numbers of wintering oldsquaw. Recent bird counts found 600 to 700 of them in the Inner Harbour and at Ashbridge's Bay.

Other wintering ducks, such as the common goldeneye and bufflehead, are found in the Inner and Outer harbours in scattered groups of up to 20. Unusual species such as the harlequin and ruddy ducks, grebes, teal, loons, scoters, American widgeon, and hooded merganser can also be seen in the Outer Harbour during the winter.

SUMMARY

The Metro Toronto waterfront has been designated by the International Joint Commission as one of 42 severely polluted areas in the Great Lakes. Although the severity of problems varies, the same ones occur across the waterfront from the Etobicoke Creek to the Rouge River. Bacterial loading causes beaches to be posted. Eutrophication is a continuing problem due to nutrient loadings. Metals and organic chemicals can be found in the water column. Bottom sediments are contaminated with organic chemicals and metals, especially in slips and embayments where water circulation is poor. Aquatic biota bio-accumulate organic chemicals and metals. Good fish habitat is scarce. Two of the worst areas along the Metro waterfront for water quality lie in the study area — the Inner Harbour and the Keating Channel. Water quality in both places is badly degraded.

Generally, water quality in the study area can be described as poor. The waters are characterized by high levels of nutrients, with the Inner Harbour bordering on a eutrophic state, and the Keating Channel already eutrophic. Levels of some metals in the Keating Channel, and occasionally the Inner and Outer harbours, exceed Provincial Water Quality Objectives. Data on organic contamination are limited. Bottom sediments are extensively contaminated throughout the waters in the study area. Benthic organisms dwelling in the bottom sediments do not appear to be bio-accumulating metals to a significant degree, but in some areas they are significantly bio-accumulating some organic compounds. The diversity of benthic organisms is directly related to pollutant levels, with the least diversity being found in the most contaminated waters, such as the Keating Channel. Because of contamination, there are restrictions on eating some sizes of six species of fish living in the Outer Harbour and Ashbridge's Bay.

The sources of these problems generally originate outside the study area. Water quality is affected by rural run-off from York Region, stormwater from the entire Don watershed, and sewage generated by hundreds of thousands of Metro Toronto residents. Atmospheric deposition brings pollutants from distant sources in Canada, the United States, and beyond. The sources of pollution from within the study area include stormwater, spills, and contaminated groundwater migrating from the soils. The relative proportions of pollution contributed by the internal sources are not known.

The reader should not assume, however, that the aquatic environment in the study area is a cause for despair. On the positive side, it must be noted that bacterial contamination is not a problem at Cherry Beach, and this beach remains one of the cleanest along the Central Waterfront in terms of bacteria. Phosphorus levels in the area and across the waterfront have been dropping over the last 15 years because of the control of phosphates in detergent and of phosphorus loadings from sewage treatment plants. The Don River, while still a major source of pollutants, is much cleaner than it was 20 years ago. It is also important to note that the Outer Harbour and Ashbridge's Bay still contain significant fish habitat, and the waters of the study area remain a major site for migrating and overwintering waterfowl. These should be considered indicators of hope, and signs that the complex problems facing the waters of the study area, and the waterfront as a whole, can be resolved.

4. THE ATMOSPHERIC ENVIRONMENT

It is often easy, even in a modern, bustling city like Toronto, to take the atmospheric environment for granted. The days of highly visible air pollution, symbolized by factories belching black smoke, are past, thanks to air pollution control laws and regulations passed in the 1970s. But there are many sources of air pollution in any urban city: automobiles, factories, hydro generating plants, and others. And on those days when people are beset by odours from a nearby plant, or our eyes sting from the high ozone levels, or warnings are issued against jogging outdoors because of air pollution, we become aware of the air we breathe, and how vital its quality is.

The atmospheric environment includes air, both indoors and out, noise, and radiation (electric and magnetic fields, as well as ionizing radiation). Outdoor, or ambient, air can be influenced by regional or greater-than-regional factors including meteorological conditions and the long-range transport of pollutants from other countries. It can also be altered by local sources — the factory ten blocks away or the neighbour with an inefficient woodstove.

This chapter describes some of the factors that affect air quality in the East Bayfront/Port Industrial Area; it is a preliminary characterization of atmospheric conditions, as determined by Phase I of the environmental audit.

LOCAL METEOROLOGICAL CONDITIONS

Weather can have a significant effect on local air quality: under good dispersion conditions, pollutants emitted rapidly disperse from a source into the atmosphere with little impact on local air quality. Some meteorological conditions, however, can adversely affect the ability of pollutants to disperse, and result in episodes of severe air pollution. Temperature and sunlight, wind, atmospheric stability, and precipitation are the meteorological factors with the greatest impact on air quality.

In the study area, the weather and dispersion conditions are influenced by geography — the close proximity of the

Influences on the atmospheric environment of the designated area include the Gardiner/Lakeshore/railway corridor, industries in and adjacent to the area, and general urban air pollution.
Courtesy of the Metropolitan Toronto and Region Conservation Authority.

urbanized Metro Toronto area to the open waters of Lake Ontario. In general, this juxtaposition encourages higher wind speeds and fewer periods of calm. The higher wind speeds help to lower pollutant concentrations from ground-level sources such as traffic. During the late spring and summer, however, differences in temperature between the city and the lake can cause periods of fumigation, where pollutants from above-ground sources such as stacks are brought close to the ground. Such periods usually cause high readings for the Air Pollution Index, which gives a measure of pollutant levels for sulphur dioxide and particulates. If the readings are high enough, the Ministry of the Environment can order sources of sulphur dioxide to curtail operations.

AMBIENT AIR QUALITY

Ambient air quality (the phrase is used to describe outdoor air quality) is usually measured by continuous air monitoring stations. Although there are none in the study area, data collected from ten monitoring stations in the vicinity, as well as special surveys of the area done in the past, make it possible to characterize ambient air quality there.

Regulation of air pollutants is largely controlled under the National Air Quality Objectives for Air Contaminants and by criteria contained in provincial Regulation 308, enacted under Ontario's *Environmental Protection Act*. These regulate acceptable concentrations of the major pollutants found in ambient air. Air pollution can affect people, vegetation, even buildings, and the provincial criteria are set for the most sensitive receptor.

The Ontario Ministry of the Environment keeps an inventory of major emitters of pollutants. Table 2 lists the study area's major emitters of sulphur dioxide, nitrogen dioxide, carbon monoxide, and volatile organic compounds. Table 3 lists major emitters in the neighbouring area for the same pollutants. The contribution of these sources relative to all sources in the Metro Toronto airshed is given.

TABLE 2

1985 Emissions in the East Bayfront and Port Industrial Area
(Tonnes)

	SO₂	NOx	CO	Particulates	VOC
Canada Malting	23.6	18.1	0.6	131.1	0.1
Commissioner St. Incin.[1]	211.0	253.0	2953.5	21.0	126.6
Compressed Metals	0.0	0.0	0.0	3.7	0.0
Darling & Co.	–	27.6	–	–	–
Lake Ontario Cement	–	–	–	3.3	–
Metro Sewage Treatment Plant	13.8	86.4	0.0	51.9	17.3
Oil Canada Co.	32.3	15.0	3.7	1.0	1.4
Paper Board Ind. (1978)	42.6	46.5	–	–	–
Redpath Sugar	84.9	90.4	4.2	11.8	1.5
Shell Canada	–	–	–	35.6	–
WMI Waste Mgt.	–	–	–	22.5	–
TOTAL	408.2	537.0	2962.0	281.9	146.9
% OF TOTAL EMISSIONS IN METRO[2]	0.7	0.5	0.6	0.9	0.1

SO2 = sulphur dioxide
NOx = nitrogen oxides
CO = carbon monoxide
VOC = volatile organic compounds
– = no information available

[1] Closed in 1985.
[2] Includes Mississauga's Lakeview Generating Station.

TABLE 3

1985 Emissions in the Neighbouring Area Influencing Air Quality in the East Bayfront and Port Industrial Area
(Tonnes)

	SO$_2$	NOx	CO	Particulates	VOC
Canada Metal	715.2	9.4	0.7	81.6	0.1
Canada Packers	18.9	10.1	0.7	45.9	119.9
Clarke A.R. Co.	1.5	170.3	34.1	0.3	56.6
Gardiner Expressway East Half	35.8	580.5	4349.2	69.2	534.8
Gooderham & Worts	3.4	15.7	1.1	1.5	0.3
Lever Bros.	62.7	80.2	4.6	41.5	1.2
Rothsay	0.5	8.0	2.0	0.2	0.2
Toronto Terminal Railway Heating	12.8	126.9	31.7	3.1	5.1
Toronto District Heating	3.2	40.9	9.9	1.5	1.6
TOTAL	854.0	1042.0	4434.0	244.8	719.8
% OF TOTAL EMISSIONS IN METRO[1]	1.4	1.0	0.8	0.8	0.4

SO2 = sulphur dioxide
NOx = nitrogen oxides
CO = carbon monoxide
VOC = volatile organic compounds

[1] Includes Mississauga's Lakeview Generating Station

Sulphur Dioxide

Sulphur dioxide is a colourless gas with a pungent odour. When combined with particulates, high levels of sulphur dioxide can affect the health of those with respiratory diseases. In the atmospheric environment, it can be a local pollutant and, when carried long distances, can form acid rain. In the 1960s and early 1970s, sulphur dioxide and particulate matter were Toronto's worst pollutants, and became the basis for the Province's Air Pollution Index. Since then, legislation controlling the sulphur content of coal and oil used in Toronto, and a large-scale switch to natural gas, have helped reduce levels of sulphur dioxide by more than 90 percent, and they are no longer a problem in the Toronto area.

The major source of sulphur dioxide for the city remains the coal-burning Lakeview Generating Plant in Mississauga, which contributes about 70 per cent of the loadings in Metro Toronto. Other major sources include automobiles, industry, and manufacturing. Measured levels at monitoring stations are well below national objectives and Ontario criteria, indicating that levels of sulphur dioxide are not a problem in the study area.

Nitrogen Dioxide

Nitrogen oxides are emitted into the atmosphere as a result of all combustion processes. Major emitters include automobiles, power plants, and incinerators. In the atmosphere, nitrogen oxides readily form nitrogen dioxide, which is a brownish gas and, at high concentrations, has a pungent odour. It is an irritant to those with asthma and bronchitis. In the last 15 years, there has been very little change in the total emissions and ambient concentrations of nitrogen dioxide in Toronto. Reductions realized as the result of improved pollution controls on motor vehicles, the Commissioner Street Incinerator closing, and the moth-balling of the Hearn

Generating Plant have been offset by increased numbers of automobiles on the streets.

Ambient levels of nitrogen dioxide *per se* are not a problem in Toronto or in the study area. However, nitrogen dioxide is a concern because of its role in producing ground-level ozone.

Carbon Monoxide

Carbon monoxide is a colourless, odourless, and tasteless gas. At levels found in the atmosphere, carbon monoxide can cause cardiovascular problems, dizziness, and headaches. The major source of carbon monoxide in the atmosphere is automobile emissions, and ambient levels are related to the amount of traffic, the average speed at which vehicles travel, and the distance from curbs.

In Toronto, exceedances of carbon monoxide still occur on some traffic arteries, although it is expected that the situation will improve as cars become more pollution control-efficient. In the study area, provincial criteria for carbon monoxide are probably exceeded in close proximity to the Gardiner Expressway and Lakeshore Boulevard, especially near exit ramps.

Volatile Organic Compounds

Volatile organic compounds are reactive hydrocarbons or compounds containing hydrogen and carbon (except for methane, which is non-reactive). They occur in the environment as a result of both natural and human sources. Among the natural reactive hydrocarbons are terpenes and isoprenes emitted by vegetation; among human sources, vehicles are by far the greatest points of origin. Other major sources in the study area include an oil refinery, fuel storage tanks and gasoline stations, rendering plants, fermentation processes, and chemical industries.

There are no national objectives or provincial criteria for this class of compounds, because their reactivity, odour, and toxicity depend on the specific compound formed. Volatile organic compounds are important precursors in the formation of ground-level ozone.

Ozone

Ozone is a colourless gas occurring naturally in the atmosphere. "High-level" ozone in the upper stratosphere is important as a screen against ultraviolet radiation from the sun. However, at ground level, high concentrations of ozone can damage vegetation and harm human health. In Southern Ontario, increases in the number of people hospitalized with respiratory disease have been correlated to high concentrations of ozone in combination with sulphates.

Ground-level ozone is formed through a complicated series of reactions involving nitrogen dioxide and volatile organic compounds in the presence of sunlight. Levels of ozone are fairly uniform across Southern Ontario, and are highest in warm, sunny weather when winds from the south and southwest bring a considerable amount of ozone-laden air from the United States. In the study area, as in the rest of Metro Toronto and Southern Ontario, ozone levels frequently exceed the national objective and provincial criteria between May and September. The frequency of exceedances is related to the number of sunny days of warm weather; it is hardly surprising, therefore, that the hot summer of 1988 was the worst on record for ozone in Toronto.

Suspended Particulate Matter

Suspended particulate matter is made up of particles small enough to remain suspended in air. They cause soiling, impair visibility, and are a nuisance. Their impact on health depends on the components of the particles and their size: smaller particles can penetrate the lungs.

The sources of suspended particulates in the study area include industrial activity generally, the sewage treatment plant, and the traffic along the Gardiner Expressway and Lakeshore Boulevard. Because suspended particulate matter is a function of local land use, it is difficult to infer the levels in the study area from monitoring stations outside. Nevertheless, it is likely that national objectives and provincial criteria for suspended particulates are exceeded in the study area, especially near the Gardiner and Lakeshore. Exceedances are also likely to occur in other locations in Metro Toronto near industrial sources.

Dustfall

Dustfall refers to heavier particles in the air which, because of their size and density, readily settle on the ground near their point of origin. As with suspended particulates, their impact depends on the components in the dustfall.

Across Metro Toronto, high levels of dustfall can be found near industrial sources where materials like sand and gravel are stored in bulk, and along major traffic arteries. In the eastern portion of the study area, dustfall from the nearby Canada Metal plant contains lead, which is particularly harmful to children. Levels of dustfall in the area are also high in the vicinity of other industries, such as the Victory Soya Mills; storage areas for coal, sand, and gravel; and near unpaved roads during dry weather. Noticeably high levels of dustfall occur along Leslie Street when trucks take fill out to the Leslie Street Spit.

High levels of dustfall also occur during dry weather in the summer and fall near the elevated Gardiner Expressway; a car parked under the expressway for a day will gather a noticeable layer of dust. During the winter and spring, there is additional dustfall caused by the suspension of salt and sand. The salt is injurious to most vegetation, its impact extending as much as 300 metres (1,000 feet) from the expressway.

Lead and Other Metals

Lead is the most common of the toxic metals in the air, mainly because it has traditionally been used as an anti-knock additive in gasoline. Because of tightening federal regulations that restricted the amount of lead in fuel, levels of lead in air have been greatly reduced in the last 15 years. However, the legacy of its use remains, with lead contamination of soil found immediately adjacent to traffic arteries, where it has been deposited over the years. In Toronto more recently, exceedances of criteria for lead in air have been found only in the vicinity of secondary lead smelters.

Levels of lead in air may exceed provincial criteria in the eastern portion of the study area because of emissions from the nearby Canada Metal plant. However, when measured for metals other than lead, ambient air quality meets provincial criteria. There are probably high levels of lead in the soil along the Gardiner Expressway and Lakeshore Boulevard as a result of deposition from traffic in the past. Lead in soils may also be found on lands previously used for gasoline storage, as scrap metal yards, and for auto-wrecking operations.

Toxic Organic Compounds

Today, we are becoming more aware of the presence of compounds in the air that are toxic — that can affect health — at extremely low concentrations. These compounds include dioxins and furans, PCBs, polycyclic aromatic hydrocarbons (PAHs), and others. As part of its study on the atmospheric deposition of chlorinated organic compounds, the Ontario Ministry of the Environment has established a monitoring station on the Toronto Islands. The object of the study is to determine the types and concentrations of trace organics in the air and precipitation, in order to understand their impact on the Great Lakes Basin.

The levels of trace organic compounds measured on the islands are similar in magnitude to those found at rural monitoring stations through Ontario. This suggests that distant sources are responsible for many of the trace organic compounds, with local sources in Metro Toronto having little impact.

The largest source of trace organic compounds in the study area is from emissions of the incinerator at the Metro Sewage

Treatment Plant. Testing in 1988 found trace levels of dioxins and furans, PCBs and PAHs, and other compounds that met provincial air quality standards. Other sources of trace organic compounds in the study area include disturbances of contaminated soil, automobile emissions, and some industrial sources such as fugitive emissions from petroleum storage tanks.

Odours

Many pollutants, chiefly sulphide and organic compounds, are very odorous in concentrations as low as a few parts per billion. As a result, they are very difficult to measure at levels that may be affecting people. Odour problems are usually identified by registering the complaints of those affected. Most are received from May to October, when people spend more time outdoors. Odours may cause nausea, headaches, loss of sleep, and emotional problems.

In Metro Toronto, odours are found in the vicinity of rendering plants, sewage treatment facilities, and some manufacturing industries. Diesel fumes from buses and trucks are also a major source. Sources of odours in the study area lie both outside and in the Port Industrial Area.

In 1986, the Ontario Ministry of the Environment conducted a special monitoring survey of the Port Industrial and South Riverdale areas to identify and quantify odorous compounds. Based on complaints, the survey in the Port area was carried out downwind of Lever Brothers, Rothsay, Oil Canada, the Darling Rendering plant, A.R. Clark, and the sewage treatment plant. Very low concentrations of odorous compounds were detected at each. While air standards were met for each specific compound, odours were noted downwind of each source and were attributed to combinations of odorous compounds.

INDOOR AIR QUALITY

Even if outside air meets air quality standards, indoor air can become a problem if poor circulation and ventilation allow pollutants to concentrate. Indoor air quality can also become a problem when buildings are constructed on land that has been used for waste deposition or an industrial activity that contaminated soil in the past. In such cases the volatile compounds emitted from the soil do not cause high levels in the outdoor air but, if they seep into buildings, concentrations inside may reach levels that affect health.

The Ontario Ministry of the Environment has established decommissioning and clean up guidelines for industrial land found to be contaminated. These guidelines require soil testing, and contain criteria for remediation and allowable land uses depending on the level of contamination.

Contamination of soil and groundwater from industrial use is extensive in the study area. (See "Soil and Groundwater" in Chapter 2.)

NOISE

Although there has been no recent study of noise in the study area, primary sources are vehicular traffic (particularly from the Gardiner/Lakeshore Corridor), railway traffic, industrial and port activities, and aircraft. In the City of Toronto, noise is regulated under a 1975 by-law that sets limits for permissible sound levels, measured in decibels.

The City of Toronto's 1976 Central Waterfront Information Base Study on the Environment concluded that the Bayfront as a whole was an area of consistently high noise levels caused by traffic sounds in the West Bayfront and a mix of traffic and industrial noise in the East Bayfront. Levels were higher in the East Bayfront than in the Port Industrial Area, where the predominant sources were industrial activities.

The Central Waterfront Study found that sound levels in the Cherry Beach area were low. Sources included wind, waves, and birds, occasional aircraft, recreational boats, and industry.

RADIATION

Two types of radiation are important in the atmospheric environment: electric and magnetic fields, and ionizing radiation. The scientific consensus is that no risk to human health from exposure to electric and magnetic fields has been established. The Ontario and Canadian governments have no guidelines for these forms of radiation. However, the World Health Organization has developed a guideline for electric fields, and the State of Florida has proposed a standard for magnetic fields. These standards are not exceeded by Ontario Hydro's transmission lines. There are no nuclear reactors in the vicinity of the study area, and nuclear radiation is at normal background levels.

SUMMARY

The air quality in the study area is affected by sources within and without. The atmospheric region of influence has been defined as extending as far away as Hudson Bay to the north, the Dakotas to the west, central Georgia to the south, and New Brunswick to the east. The levels of some pollutants — ozone and toxic organic compounds — are affected chiefly by distant sources in the United States. The levels of sulphur dioxide and nitrogen dioxide are influenced mostly by regional sources, and differ very little across Metro Toronto.

The pollutant levels influenced most by sources in, or just adjacent to, the study area are carbon monoxide, suspended particulate, dustfall, lead, and odours.

Aspects of the current atmospheric environment in the East Bayfront/Port Industrial Area can be characterized as poor, and typical of an industrial area — this, despite the fact that levels of some primary pollutants are quite acceptable. Levels of sulphur dioxide and nitrogen dioxide, in particular, are not a problem in the study area, or in the rest of Metro Toronto.

However, like the West Bayfront, the entire area is subject to high noise levels from road and rail traffic, industry, and aircraft, with those in the East Bayfront being higher than in the Port Industrial Area. As in other areas of Metro near certain kinds of industries, odours are a problem, caused both from sources inside the study area and from those adjacent to it. The impact of these odours is felt, not only in the study area, but also in nearby residential areas (e.g., South Riverdale).

During warm daytime hours in the late spring and summer, ground-level ozone is a problem in the study area, as it is in the rest of Metro Toronto and Southern Ontario. Standards for dustfall and suspended particulates are probably exceeded throughout the area, with conditions being worst along the Gardiner/Lakeshore Corridor. Such exceedances are noted in other areas of Metro that lie close to industries where materials like sand and gravel are stored in bulk, and in those areas close to high-traffic arteries.

Near the Gardiner and Lakeshore, provincial criteria for carbon monoxide are exceeded. Lead in air and in dustfall is a problem in the eastern part of the area because of the nearby Canada Metal plant. High levels of lead in soil from past automobile emissions probably occur along the Gardiner and Lakeshore, as along other major traffic arteries.

Because of soil contamination in the area, indoor air quality may be adversely affected. This may also be true in other parts of Metro where similar industrial activities occurred and redevelopment has been carried out without prior soil remediation.

5. STEWARDSHIP AND ACCOUNTABILITY

Governments play a major role in determining the state of the environment of the East Bayfront/Port Industrial Area. However, that role is characterized by gaps and overlaps of responsibility between different governments and different agencies. There is no single government level or agency responsible for environmental management in the East Bayfront/Port Industrial Area.

The legal framework comprises statutes, regulations, guidelines, and policies promulgated by the federal and Ontario governments, as well as by-laws of the relevant municipalities. It is complicated by shared constitutional authority among various levels of governments.

Governments' influence over the designated area is especially strong because so much of the land is publicly owned. The government bodies with stewardship of these lands have special accountability for many of the environmental conditions described in this report.

Some major federal ministries present in the study area include the departments of Environment, Public Works, Transport, and Fisheries and Oceans. The Government of Canada has jurisdiction over navigation, shipping, fisheries, harbour activities, and, to some extent, water quality.

The Board of Toronto Harbour Commissioners (THC), which was created by federal statute, is also an important factor. It is a major landholder with responsibility for operating the Port and developing the land under its stewardship.

The provincial presence in the area includes the ministries of Environment, Natural Resources, and Municipal Affairs, which have various responsibilities with respect to air, soil, and water quality, wetlands, fisheries, and municipal planning.

Municipalities with authority in the study area are the Municipality of Metropolitan Toronto, which establishes overall planning direction and regulates sewer use, and the

City of Toronto, which has responsibility for planning, zoning, and building. The Metropolitan Toronto and Region Conservation Authority, which works as a provincial-municipal partnership, was established under the *Conservation Authorities Act*, which empowers it to develop, implement, and co-ordinate watershed management plans. MTRCA's waterfront planning authority is limited because it has no say on Toronto's Central Waterfront.

In addition to the City of Toronto and Metropolitan Toronto, the other municipalities with jurisdiction in the Don River watershed — the Regional Municipality of York and the municipalities of East York, North York, Scarborough, Vaughan, Markham, and Richmond Hill — are also accountable for some environmental conditions in the area.

This chapter considers the basis for governmental action affecting the quality of the environment on the study lands. A brief review, it is intended as a starting point in exploring how agencies operate in practice and, more important, which ones can be held accountable for the state of the environment in the area.

THE CONSTITUTIONAL CONTEXT

Authority to legislate environmental matters was not explicitly attributed to either the federal or provincial governments by the Constitution Act of 1867. It gave the provinces broad legislative powers to affect the environment by virtue of their ownership of lands and other natural resources within their own boundaries and through such specific categories of legislative power as authority over local works and undertakings. In addition, provinces were empowered to create municipalities and delegate to them any of the powers the provinces had received under section 92 of the Constitution. Because municipalities are creatures of the Province, the scope of their authority is limited by provincial law.

Federal powers over shipping, harbours, fisheries, and criminal law, all specifically assigned under the Constitution, have been used to support environmental legislation. In addition to those specifically given, the federal government has the power to pass laws for the "Peace, Order and good Government of Canada", on which it may rely in limited circumstances. These include national emergencies, matters arising that did not exist in 1867, and issues of national concern, such as pollution extending beyond provincial boundaries.

THE REGULATORY FRAMEWORK

Overview

By and large, the regulatory framework governing the environment of the East Bayfront/Port Industrial Area is made up of different, and sometimes overlapping, instruments for air quality, surface and groundwater quality, site decommissioning and clean-up, natural heritage, and the built environment. There is no legal instrument that deals comprehensively with the various components of the study area in particular, or of the environment in general. The framework is composed of laws and other instruments intended to protect the environment and those directed at land use planning.

An important element in environmental protection is environmental impact assessment. Projects on federal lands, those initiated or funded by federal departments, and those for which there is federal decision-making authority must comply with the 1984 federal *Environmental Assessment and Review Guidelines Order*. It requires the department initiating a project to carry out an "initial environmental evaluation" of the potential impact on the environment and, if that is likely to be significant, requires that a panel be convened to review a full environmental impact statement. The public can participate in the review, which results only in a set of recommendations to the responsible minister.

Until recent court decisions established that compliance with the Order was mandatory (in cases involving the Alameda – Rafferty Dam in Saskatchewan and the Oldman River Dam in Alberta), it was not often fully observed. Although the THC is not required to comply with the *Federal Environmental Assessment and Review Process* (EARP), it voluntarily undertook an initial assessment for the Outer Harbour Marina. Proposed changes to the EARP may clarify the issue of compliance by the THC.

Most provincial and municipal projects must follow Ontario's *Environmental Assessment Act*. Private-sector projects can be required to submit to an environmental assessment (as happened with the proposed Trintek energy-from-waste plant on the waterfront). The *Act* requires that the proponent evaluate the environmental impact of a project and of possible alternatives. The evaluation is submitted for broad governmental review and public comment and, very often, a public hearing is held before the Environmental Assessment Board. The board (or, if there is no hearing, the Minister of the Environment) must approve the project before it can proceed.

Air Quality

There is legislation governing air quality at both the federal and provincial levels. Federally, the *Canadian Environmental Protection Act 1985, amended 1989* (CEPA) provides federal ministers of the Environment and of Health and Welfare the authority to control and regulate many aspects of environmental protection; however, few specific or enforceable standards or controls have been established. National Ambient Air Quality Objectives have been set for several common pollutants. Although they are objectives only, and therefore unenforceable, they are intended to encourage uniformity in provincial air quality laws and regulations.

The federal government also has power to set enforceable emission standards for stationary sources (e.g., the Secondary

Lead Smelter National Emission Standards Regulations) and for emissions from new motor vehicles.

New federal regulations may also result from the assessment of pollutants on the Priority Substances List that is part of *CEPA*. For example, the assessment report for dioxins and furans has led to recommendations that regulations for incinerators be developed.

Provincially, Ontario's *Environmental Protection Act* (*EPA*) authorizes the Province to adopt measures to protect and conserve the natural environment. Regulations passed under it deal with control of air pollution from industrial sources, air quality criteria, vehicle emissions, ferrous foundries, asphalt paving plants, and the sulphur content of fuel consumed in Metro Toronto.

Under the *EPA*, approval from the Ministry of the Environment (MOE) is needed before facilities that release pollutants into the air can be built or modified. A Certificate of Approval, which permits the control technology to be used, can be obtained only after dischargers satisfy the MOE that they can meet the air quality standards in Regulation 308 and that they will not violate the general prohibition on discharging contaminants into the natural environment. Public hearings are not required before certificates of approval for air pollution sources can be issued, but public meetings are now held as a matter of MOE policy.

In addition, the MOE has established policies and guidelines for the control of many types of industrial sources and specific pollutants. There are two policies and a guideline that are particularly relevant to the Port Industrial Area: the 1987 policy prescribing combustion conditions and emission controls for energy from waste incinerators; the policy statement requiring private sector energy from waste (EFW) facilities to be designated under the *Environmental Assessment Act*; and the 1973 Guidelines for Buffer Zones Surrounding Sewage Treatment Plants, which attempt to reduce exposure to odours.

The MOE is proposing to overhaul current air pollution laws through its Clean Air Program (CAP), which will fundamentally change all regulation of air pollution by replacing the air quality standards in Regulation 308 with bottom-of-the-stack emission limits. Dischargers will be able to meet these limits in any way they choose, but different levels of technology will be required, depending on the toxicity or other characteristics of the emissions. The revised regulation will contain updated air pollution models, including one relevant to the waterfront area, designed especially for sources located along a lakeshore. Revisions were first proposed in 1983 and a discussion paper on CAP was released in 1987. Since then, no further documents have been circulated for public review.

Surface Water Quality

Like those related to air quality, water quality laws exist both federally and provincially. The federal *Fisheries Act* provides a mechanism by which the Government of Canada can control discharges of effluents. Unless they are authorized by the Minister of the Environment substances may not be discharged into waters if they could be harmful to fish or fish habitat, and the Department of the Environment can require plans for undertakings that might have harmful effects.

Under this *Act*, the federal government has the power to establish effluent standards for specific pollutants. Despite the broad nature of these powers, the *Act* is poorly enforced. In order to overcome the problem, the DOE is developing a new Enforcement and Compliance Policy, to be released sometime this year.

Part XX of the *Canada Shipping Act* has sewage regulations that are applicable to discharges from vessels.

The Canadian Council of Ministers of the Environment (CCME), in its earlier manifestation as the Canadian Council of Resource and Environment Ministers, developed and promoted Canadian Water Quality Guidelines for major water uses including drinking water, recreational water quality and aesthetics, freshwater aquatic life, agricultural uses, and industrial uses.

Ontario used the Ministry of the Environment's "Blue Book" on Water Management as the primary tool for protecting water quality. The book sets out the goals, policies, objectives, and implementation procedures for managing surface and groundwater quality and quantity. Water Quality Objectives are used to set effluent standards, which are then incorporated into certificates of approval, granted under the *Ontario Water Resources Act (OWRA)*, which deals with establishing or modifying wastewater treatment plants.

In 1986, the MOE initiated a Municipal/Industrial Strategy for Abatement (MISA) program aimed at controlling municipal and industrial discharges into surface waters. Regulations have been enacted to require industrial facilities that discharge directly into surface waters to monitor and report their wastewater discharges. Regulations are now being developed that will require dischargers to meet effluent standards that can be attained by using the best available pollution abatement technology that is "economically achievable". Once effluent limits have been set, emphasis will shift to developing water quality standards that protect receiving waters.

MISA has also undertaken a number of programs pertaining to discharges to sewers and will eventually require all such dischargers to employ the best available control technology economically achievable.

In the meantime, municipalities use by-laws to regulate industry discharges into municipal sewer systems. Many Ontario communities, including Metropolitan Toronto, have their own sewer use by-laws and enforcement officers.

The Metropolitan Toronto and Region Conservation Authority (MTRCA) has few powers relevant to water quality. MTRCA's only related authority in the study area is in implementing the Improved Lakefill Quality Control Program.

Dredging activities can also affect water quality. The MOE has issued dredging guidelines, which Environment Canada has applied to federal dredging projects undertaken by the Department of Public Works, the Toronto Harbour Commissioners, and Harbourfront Corporation. New proposed provincial sediment quality guidelines are now under federal and provincial review.

The MTRCA's program of dredging the Keating Channel and of dredgeate disposal was subject to environmental review under the provincial *Environmental Assessment Act*.

Groundwater Quality

Provincial water quality objectives are relevant, not only to the management of surface waters, but also to groundwater quality. In addition, groundwater quality objectives have been established for human drinking water use and for agricultural use, including irrigation. MOE policy is aimed at reducing or preventing contamination of groundwater by proposed or existing regulated and unregulated activities, such as spills and leaks, and from industrial sites such as those in the Port Industrial Area.

The MOE's policy for addressing unregulated sources of groundwater contamination provides only that "all reasonable measures shall be undertaken to reduce or prevent the contamination of ground water from such sources".

Site Decommissioning and Clean-up

There are no formal laws dealing specifically with site decommissioning and clean-up in Canada. Instead, Environment Canada and the MOE approach each project on a case-by-case basis. There are draft national guidelines for decommissioning industrial sites, which include planning requirements, a phased approach to decommissioning, and an approach for development of clean-up criteria. The guidelines do not recommend specific clean-up criteria for industrial sites.

In February 1989, the MOE released *Guidelines for the Decommissioning and Clean-up of Sites in Ontario*, in order to provide a common framework for clean-ups in the province. Although the guidelines are unenforceable, the MOE has authority, arising from the provisions of the *EPA*, to ensure that a clean-up is undertaken and is conducted in a way that will minimize environmental harm. However, it is not clear that the MOE has any legal authority over federal lands.

Basically, the MOE guidelines involve four phases: 1) planning a clean-up; 2) designing and implementing a clean-up plan; 3) verification of clean-up; and 4) signing off the clean-up. There are clean-up criteria for selected metals, pH, and oil and grease, but not for organic compounds such as benzene, phenols or PAHs. The guidelines also suggest that clean-up criteria above background levels may be developed, provided that they protect human health and the environment.

In addition, the *Occupational Health and Safety Act* may be applied to protect people involved in clean-up projects or working in buildings constructed on contaminated lands. The *Act* sets exposure limits for more than 400 organic and inorganic compounds.

The *EPA* requires that ministerial approval be obtained before land can be used, if, in the past 25 years, it has been used for waste disposal. Regulations deem soils with PCB concentrations of more than 50 parts per million to be PCB waste and to require special disposal sites. Ontario has also recently adopted PCB interim soil guidelines and guidelines for contamination of soil and groundwater at abandoned coal tar sites. The latter may be relevant to the former coal tar distillation and briquetting plants located in the designated area.

Under its planning process, the City of Toronto has the opportunity to include environmental guidelines and policies in site plan applications, severances, rezoning applications, and official plan amendments.

Natural Heritage

A number of legislative and policy mechanisms are aimed at protecting wildlife and their habitats. The federal *Migratory Birds Convention Act* is designed to protect migratory birds and, to a lesser extent, their habitats. While weaknesses in the way the *Act* was drafted have reduced its effectiveness, it has, on occasion, proven to be useful. For example, the federal Department of the Environment recently invoked the *Act* to prevent the Hamilton Harbour Commission from disturbing common terns nesting on some dikework.

By contrast, the federal *Fisheries Act* could become one of the most powerful tools available to governments attempting to protect fish habitat. The federal *Act* is implemented in part by the provinces, but clearly gives the federal government wide authority to protect fish habitat through its approval and enforcement powers. Yet these sweeping powers are rarely used.

In 1986, the federal government produced a policy for managing fish habitat, including strategies to achieve habitat protection. The policy is meant to prevent a net loss in habitat by conserving what already exists, restoring what has been damaged, and developing new habitat.

The federal Department of Fisheries and Oceans is currently trying to develop priorities for managing fish habitat in areas under the jurisdiction of harbour commissions. Areas critical for habitat protection would be identified and classified according to their importance as fish habitat.

As part of the 1988 joint Canada-Ontario Fisheries Agreement, the Ontario Ministry of Natural Resources is currently developing a Strategic Plan for Ontario Fisheries known as SPOF II. The idea is to develop an ecosystem approach to help protect healthy aquatic ecosystems and rehabilitate those that are now degraded.

The Ontario *Planning Act* offers the Municipality of Metropolitan Toronto and the City of Toronto some possibility of protecting natural heritage in parts of the study area. The Metro Official Plan provides guidance for official plans in its constituent municipalities and, therefore, the City of Toronto Official Plan must be consistent with it. The provisions of official plans are then implemented through city zoning by-laws. The Metro Official Plan includes a "Valley Land Impact Zone", which is designed to restrict development in flood- or erosion-prone areas. It may also be used to help maintain natural and environmentally sensitive areas. Recommendations have been made to strengthen this planning tool.

The City of Toronto has developed a plan, still awaiting approval from the Minister of Municipal Affairs, which includes official plan amendments for the Central Waterfront. The Central Waterfront Plan, adopted by the City of Toronto Council in June 1988, includes policies for Environmental Resource Areas (ERAs) on the Leslie Street Spit and Toronto Islands. These are defined as sites that contain unusual, rare, significant or sensitive environmental features and are to be maintained and managed for conservation, public enjoyment, and compatible recreation uses.

The plan also includes proposals for two new open space zones, one of which would permit parks, marinas, and related uses (Gm), and the other to be applied to specific open space areas and waterlots (Gr). In the designated area, the second type of zone is proposed for much of the north shore of the Outer Harbour, the THC's Outer Harbour Marina, and the Outer Harbour's waterlots.

Built Heritage

Two provincial statutes deal directly with preserving the built environment: the *Ontario Heritage Act* and the *Planning Act*. The purpose of the *Heritage Act* is to protect significant historic, architectural, and archaeological resources. It empowers municipalities to include heritage in an official plan and, under Part IV, to identify and maintain a registry of important buildings. Part V permits municipalities to create heritage conservation districts and to establish guidelines for protecting the characters of those districts.

In the City of Toronto, properties designated under Part IV cannot be altered or demolished without application for a permit and a review by the Toronto Historical Board. Changes that are not in keeping with a building's history must be approved by City Council. Similarly, a heritage permit approved by City Council is required for alterations, additions, and demolition in heritage conservation districts. Throughout Ontario, municipal councils seek advice on heritage issues from the Local Architectural Conservation Advisory Committee (LACAC).

Despite these powers, demolition of a heritage building cannot be permanently enjoined by a municipality, only delayed for 180 days. Individual buildings in heritage conservation districts cannot be designated, which suggests that they are less protected under this form of preservation. It is not possible to designate heritage landscapes or land owned by the provincial or federal governments. The *Ontario Heritage Act* is currently under review, in order to address some of these concerns.

Section 2 of the *Planning Act* stipulates that the Minister of Municipal Affairs must be cognizant of and respect heritage resources, but the *Act's* real strength is that it empowers municipalities to establish an official plan and zoning restrictions. Zoning differs from historic designation because it tends to be broad-brushed — i.e., permissible uses and restrictions in an area are established under which each property owner is treated like any other with the same zoning. An application cannot be refused as long as it complies with established zoning. However, zoning can preserve buildings by restricting uses, establishing design guidelines, and limiting development over broad areas.

SUMMARY

This snapshot is of the regulatory framework as it stands at this time. Although it is focused on a relatively small geographic area — the East Bayfront/Port Industrial Area — it can be viewed as a paradigm for other areas in Ontario and even across Canada.

The laws, policies, and guidelines governing environmental quality in the study area are complex and in a state of flux, with a variety of federal and provincial initiatives under way to make improvements.

The existing regulatory framework is characterized by overlap and duplication by different levels of government, by joint action on some issues, and by failure to exercise authority that is already in place. Many aspects of environmental protection depend on guidelines and policies rather than enforceable regulations. The framework is fragmented, with different instruments governing separate aspects of the environment — which makes it difficult to apply ecosystem goals and principles.

The roles and responsibilities of regulatory agencies, landholders, and tenants are not always clear. A more detailed review of the regulatory framework is necessary to fully explore the issues of stewardship and accountability for the state of the environment in the study area.

6. THE PHASE II PROGRAM

During Phase I of the environmental audit of the East Bayfront/Port Industrial Area, an attempt was made to review all existing sources of information on its terrestrial, aquatic, and atmospheric environments. Because of a lack of participation by the City of Toronto and the Toronto Harbour Commissioners during that phase, some information was not available to the environmental audit work groups.

The Phase I review of existing, accessible information revealed a number of gaps in our knowledge about the environment of the study area. This chapter summarizes these gaps and suggests some options for research programs that might fill them. Some of the suggested research will be undertaken as Phase II of the environmental audit. Other research may become part of existing or future programs of other agencies (e.g., the Metro Toronto Remedial Action Plan, the Clean Air Program, and others).

Because some of these programs could be in existence longer than the environmental audit, certain aspects of the research may not be complete by the end of Phase II.

AN ECOSYSTEM APPROACH

During Phase I of the environmental audit, the study area was investigated by separating the environment into five components: air, water, land, built heritage, and natural heritage. To apply an ecosystem approach however, it is necessary to focus on *relationships* among the various elements of the environment, including humans. Although the Phase I research did reveal some ecosystem interactions (see Chapter 7), more work is needed to develop a better understanding of how the ecosystem in the study area functions.

Because the Phase II research program will be designed to focus on *interactions* among land, air, water, and living organisms, including humans, it might deal with such questions as:

- What chemicals and materials are being brought into the area and/or are being produced in it and what risks do they entail?

- Are contaminants being transferred among the soils, groundwater, surface waters, and air, and, if so, what is the relative importance of such transfers?

- What effects do the environmental conditions have on human health, behaviour, access, activities, and decision-making?

- What is the impact of the environmental conditions on wildlife diversity, abundance, and health ?

- What measures are necessary to protect and restore beneficial uses?

- What regional relationships exist between the environment of the study area and that in downtown Toronto, the Greater Toronto Area, the Great Lakes, etc.?

PROGRAM OPTIONS

Within the broad framework of an ecosystem approach, some specific gaps in our information base and related research options include:

1. Human Health

Little information was gathered in Phase I about the possible impact of the contaminants in environment on human health. A better understanding of the implications of air pollution, soil contamination, water quality impairments, etc., would be useful in assessing the suitability of the area for future uses, and in determining appropriate methods and levels of environmental remediation.

Research Option: a review of existing information about the impact on human health of the types of environmental conditions found in the study area.

2.   Quality of Life

The environmental review undertaken in Phase I stimulated several questions about the quality of the environment for people using the area for work or recreation. As noted in earlier chapters, parts of the East Bayfront/Port Industrial Area create quite different experiences for people. On one hand, the open spaces adjacent to the lake offer views, cool summer breezes, and opportunities to see wildlife. On the other, much of the industrial area is perceived as noisy, barren, smelly, and dusty — not a place to enjoy being outside.

Research Option: recognizing that "quality of life" can encompass many factors, an environmental audit of this aspect would focus on issues associated with outdoor environmental conditions. It would help in gaining a better appreciation of 1) values, and how they might be enhanced, and 2) problems, and possible solutions.

3.   Assessment of Built Heritage

As described in chapters 1 and 2, an understanding of the built heritage of the study area will be important in ensuring that, as further changes occur in the area, they are undertaken with respect for the built heritage. The Phase I review revealed a good understanding of the historical context and development of the East Bayfront/Port Industrial Area. The next step is a detailed assessment of the built heritage. The THC is currently undertaking such an assessment in the Port Industrial Area, but not in the East Bayfront.

Research Option: once published, the THC's assessment of built heritage in the Port Industrial Area can be incorporated into the database for Phase II of the environmental audit. An assessment of the built heritage of the East Bayfront would provide a complete picture of built heritage for the entire audit study area.

4.   Soils and Groundwater

During Phase I, information about the current soil and groundwater conditions was obtained by reviewing site histories and examining available decommissioning and geotechnical studies. The studies contained data on petroleum refinery and storage sites, a former foundry, and a former coal tar distillation plant. No studies were available to the Royal Commission regarding sites used for other activities that might be expected to cause contamination of soils and/or groundwater: metal recycling, chemical storage, hydro substations or incinerator ash disposal.

Although the available studies were useful, they were, in some cases, incomplete. For example, the investigation of the former foundry site provides details on soil chemistry but nothing about groundwater, whereas the report on a former fuel storage facility contains information on groundwater but not on soil chemistry.

Lists of possible contaminants for which sampling was done vary from site to site, ranging from very complete to very limited. They were often chosen on the basis of the Provincial Guidelines for the Decommissioning and Clean-up of Sites in Ontario, which do not include specific organic contaminants.

Existing site-specific studies showed the presence of groundwater contaminated with oil and grease, phenols, metals, and volatile hydrocarbons. However, there is little information on the possible migration of contaminated groundwater to adjacent sites or to surface waters.

There is limited experience with remediation techniques in Ontario. However, Environment Canada is leading a major program at the federal Wastewater Technology Centre to develop and test remediation techniques on the Vancouver waterfront. The results of this program will be applied to similar industrial sites across the country.

Research Options: to obtain a better understanding of soil and groundwater conditions in the study area, Phase II of the environmental audit could include:

- a review of additional geotechnical and geochemical information from industries that have already offered to provide studies to the environmental audit, as well as from companies that may decide to participate during Phase II;

- a soil and groundwater testing program that might include sites where contamination is expected — such as those formerly or now used for petroleum storage and distribution, metal recycling, primary metals, chemical storage, transformer substations, incinerator ash disposal, and areas near the Gardiner/Lakeshore Corridor. In addition, tests could be done of sites where residual contamination from industrial activities is *not* expected, which could possibly provide baseline information for comparison with more contaminated locations. It might also reveal contamination from other sources, such as from materials used in lakefilling and/or from migration of polluted groundwater;

- a review of decommissioning and clean-up guidelines used in Ontario and in other jurisdictions to determine the most appropriate approaches for evaluating different contamination problems in relation to potential land uses in the study area;

- a review of possible remediation techniques, including on-site treatment, excavation, and removal, and off-site treatment;

- an investigation of possible contributions of contaminants from groundwater to the lake and the potential impact on aquatic habitats and recreational water use;

- an investigation of possible transfers of contaminants and suspended particulates to the atmosphere from wind-blown soil and dust;

- a review of the potential for transfer of volatile contaminants from soils and/or groundwater into buildings and the implications for indoor air quality.

5.   Biological Inventory

Phase I of the environmental audit yielded excellent information on birds and butterflies, but limited data on other kinds of terrestrial wildlife. Although there is good material on fish species and habitats in Ashbridge's Bay and the Leslie Street Spit, there is nothing recent about the Outer Harbour.

One of the most important values of the study area for wildlife is as a location for feeding and resting during migration of birds and butterflies. The size and habitat diversity of migration staging areas are important factors in their ability to successfully provide for the needs of different species of birds. It is important to consider the adequacy of staging areas along the northern shore of Lake Ontario in relation to the capacity and location of other wildlife refuges along the migratory flyways.

Further information on terrestrial and aquatic wildlife in the study area would be useful 1) in identifying specific areas for habitat conservation; and 2) in developing restoration, enhancement, and management programs for wildlife and their habitat.

Research Options: surveys of plants, reptiles, amphibians, fish, and mammals including species inventories and habitat requirements.

6.   Water Quality

There is limited information on water quality in the study area. Because of differences in sampling sites, sampling periods, methods used, and parameters for which analysis was done, it is difficult to accurately assess trends over time. In particular, data on contaminant levels of organic chemicals are poor.

Research Option: a comprehensive program of water quality monitoring in the study area.

7. Sediment Loading from the Don River

The estimated annual loading of sediments (including contaminants) from the Don River is based largely on models that have not been verified. It is not known, for example, if the recent development boom in York Region has caused significant increases in total loading of contaminants and sediments, or if relative loadings to the Don from particular upstream sources have changed.

Research Option: a program to quantify sediment and contaminant loading from the Don River.

8. Sewers Discharging to the Harbour

Although there are data on bacterial loadings to the Inner Harbour from storm sewers and combined storm-sewer overflows, little is known about inputs of metals and organic contaminants from these sources.

Research Option: a program to determine the loadings of metals and organic chemicals to the Inner Harbour from storm sewers and combined storm-sewer overflows.

9. Toxicity of Sediments to Aquatic Biota

While data exist on the contaminant levels in bottom sediments in the study area, there is no specific information on the toxicity of these sediments to aquatic life.

Research Option: a program of bioassays conducted on biota from benthic (bottom-dwelling) communities in order to determine the toxicity of bottom sediments to these organisms.

10. Air Quality Modelling

For modelling purposes, accurate predictions of the impact of the atmospheric environment on proposed land use and *vice versa* require accurate information on meteorology and sources of pollutants. The Ministry of the Environment has recently developed a new model for waterfront areas and will include it in modifications to Regulation 308.

Research Options: a program to collect data and develop an accurate model of the atmospheric environment in the study area. This might include:

- updating the emission inventory using recent tests and factors for all sources of air pollution that have an impact on the area;

- recording and improving the quality assurance program of the measurements of wind speed and direction taken at the station on the Outer Headland;

- carrying out air quality modelling for the area, using the above information, recent traffic data, and recently validated highway models.

11. Impact of the Gardiner/Lakeshore Corridor

It is expected that levels of some pollutants will exceed provincial criteria in the vicinity of the Gardiner/Lakeshore corridor. Assessing the quality of ambient air in the area and determining the extent of the area affected would be a useful planning tool.

Research Option: air surveys at various distances from the Gardiner/Lakeshore Corridor, to assess the ambient air quality and confirm model predictions.

12. Toxics in Ambient Air

Although it is believed that levels of toxic chemicals in the air are not a problem in the study area, it encompasses many potential sources of such chemicals.

Research Option: air quality surveys of toxics, especially those noted in the emission tests of the Sewage Treatment Plant incinerator, to assess levels of toxics and confirm model predictions.

13. Noise

The study area has been described as noisy. Information on noise levels there is old, however, and needs to be updated.

Research Option: a comprehensive survey of the area to determine sources, distribution, diurnal and seasonal variations, and levels of noise.

14. Odours

There are sources of odours both in and outside the study area. It is not known whether industrial sources are using best available technology to control emissions of odorous compounds.

Research Option: a program to ascertain whether sources of odours are using best available technology and good management practices.

15. Stewardship and Accountability

The environmental regulatory framework is based on a collection of laws, regulations, policies, and guidelines pertaining to different aspects of the environment and administered by different levels of government. During Phase I of the environmental audit, we gained a preliminary insight into the complexity, overlapping responsibilities, and inadequacies of the regulatory framework.

Research Option: further research to explore the issues of stewardship and accountability in relation to the environment of the study area. It might investigate such questions as:

- What responsibilities should accompany stewardship of the land?

- How could accountability for environmental protection be clarified and strengthened?

- How could an ecosystem approach be applied to the regulatory framework?

- What changes are needed to make the regulatory framework more effective?

7. SYNTHESIS

ENVIRONMENTAL CONDITIONS IN THE EAST BAYFRONT/PORT INDUSTRIAL AREA

The historical background of the East Bayfront/Port Industrial Area explains many of today's conditions: it was created by filling Ashbridge's Bay, a delta marsh at the mouth of the Don River, once famous throughout eastern North America for its abundant wildlife. Although the wetlands have been destroyed, a great diversity of birds still migrates through the area, stopping to rest and feed in the semi-wild areas along the north shore of the Outer Harbour.

The Toronto Harbour Commissioners' 1912 plan for waterfront development was a major determinant in shaping the landform, shoreline, and uses of the East Bayfront/Port Industrial Area. Built heritage there reflects the intentions of the 1912 plan: a strong framework of dockwalls, channels, roads, and railways are the setting for ships, oil tanks, warehouses, factories, and the like. This legacy recalls an important phase in Toronto's economic history. Future redevelopment should respect the port and industrial heritage, to maintain a sense of continuity with the past and sustain collective memories of our history.

The predominant uses of the study area were, and in many cases still are, petroleum product refining, storage and distribution, metal refining, manufacturing and recycling, coal storage, tar distillation, and food processing. Not surprisingly, the industrial character of this part of Toronto has given it a reputation of environmental degradation. It is generally assumed that air, water, and soils there are polluted and unhealthy.

The Phase I review of environmental conditions suggests that soils and groundwater in many parts of the area are indeed contaminated — a legacy of industrial activities and, in some cases, of lakefilling with contaminated materials. Soil and/or groundwater quality data were available for 13 of the

123 sites in the East Bayfront/Port Industrial Area. At many of the sites where soil quality data were available, volatile organics (e.g., benzene, toluene, xylene), polycyclic aromatic hydrocarbons (PAHs), oil, grease, and heavy metals were found. At most of the sites, some samples exceeded the lower explosive limit for soil gas, provincial decommissioning guidelines for oil and grease, and at least one of the health-related metal parameters (cadmium, lead or mercury). Groundwater analyses showed the presence of free product (petroleum products that sit on top of groundwater), as well as levels of phenols, volatile organics, and heavy metals above Provincial Water Quality Objectives. Areas with contaminated soils and groundwater will require remediation before any redevelopment can occur.

In contrast, the unmanaged vegetation of areas *not* used for industry — the vacant lots, the north shore of the Outer Harbour, and the base of the spit — supports many species of birds, butterflies and other invertebrates, reptiles, amphibians, and mammals. These areas are particularly valuable to migrating birds and butterflies, especially the monarch butterfly. The wildlife can be enjoyed by naturalists, cyclists, and joggers on the Martin Goodman Trail, sailors at the North Shore Clubs, picnickers at Cherry Beach, and others.

The East Bayfront/Port Industrial Area lies in the Toronto Waterfront Area of Concern, identified by the International Joint Commission for remedial action due to water quality impairment. Most of the water bodies in the study area have poor water quality, when measured in terms of nutrient enrichment, clarity, and the presence of contaminants including heavy metals and organic compounds. Waters and sediments in the Keating and Ship channels and in the Inner Harbour tend to be the most highly polluted. Ashbridge's Bay and the Outer Harbour generally meet provincial objectives for some parameters, but not for others.

The quality of water and sediments in the study area is influenced primarily by sources outside it, especially discharges from the Don River watershed, from the Metro Toronto Main Sewage Treatment Plant (which services a considerable portion of Metro Toronto), and storm-sewer outfalls along the shoreline. The review of existing information on the aquatic environment did not enable us to characterize possible contributions from the study area itself — for example, via groundwater or from storm sewers draining the industrial area.

Notwithstanding its water quality problems, the study area does include one of the cleanest swimming beaches (Cherry Beach on the Outer Harbour) in Metro Toronto, as measured by the presence of fecal coliform bacteria. The Outer Harbour is generally not exposed to the primary sources of bacterial pollution: the Don River and discharges of partially treated stormwater and sewage that occur when the Sewage Treatment Plant's capacity is exceeded following major rainfalls.

Aquatic wildlife is affected by the poor water quality and by the limited habitat structure of the water bodies in the area. Diversity of bottom-dwelling invertebrates and fish species is low, particularly in the Keating and Ship channels and the Inner Harbour. Better quality habitat in the embayments of the Leslie Street Spit and Ashbridge's Bay Park supports a greater variety and abundance of fish. Despite the polluted water and sediments, large concentrations of waterfowl overwinter in the waters of the Keating Channel, the harbour, and the sewage lagoons.

The atmospheric environment of the study area is influenced not only by sources in and near the area, but by regional and distant sources. For example, ground-level ozone is a problem throughout Southern Ontario during warm weather in spring and summer. The Gardiner/Lakeshore Corridor creates a linear zone of relatively high pollution levels, especially of carbon monoxide, dustfall, and suspended particulates. Elevated levels of lead probably occur in the soils adjacent to the traffic corridor — a legacy from decades of the use of leaded gasoline. Levels of trace organic compounds are similar to those found throughout Southern Ontario, suggesting that local sources are probably insignificant as a problem when compared to long-range transport.

Air pollution resulting from industrial activities in and adjacent to the Port Industrial Area includes dustfall and suspended particulates, lead, and odours. Contamination of indoor air may occur as a result of volatile compounds leaking from polluted soils. The entire study area is subjected to noise from road and rail traffic, industry, and aircraft.

TOWARDS AN ECOSYSTEM APPROACH

Phase I of the environmental audit was undertaken in order to gain a preliminary understanding of all aspects of the environment in the identified area — terrestrial, aquatic, and atmospheric. This represents a fairly typical approach to dividing complex ecosystems for analysis. However, it is important to recognize that there are many links and interactions among these major aspects of the environment. In addition, humans, as part of the ecosystem, have an impact on the terrestrial, aquatic, and atmospheric environments and are, in turn, influenced by environmental conditions.

Therefore, during Phase I we began to identify interactions among different environmental processes and conditions, and tried to understand the roles of human activities. The Phase II research program will be designed to develop the ecosystem approach further. This will entail interdisciplinary application of scientific concepts and methods in order to explore links, to understand how the various parts of the ecosystem fit together, and to identify management options intended to restore ecosystem integrity.

Some of the major links between and among humans and different factors in the environment are illustrated in Figure 7. If we can develop an understanding of the relative significance of the major links and flows, as well as of the individual environmental factors themselves, we will be in a better

FIGURE 7:

SCHEMATIC DIAGRAM OF THE PRIMARY LINKAGES AMONG HUMANS AND MAJOR ENVIRONMENTAL COMPARTMENTS – EAST BAYFRONT AND PORT INDUSTRIAL AREA

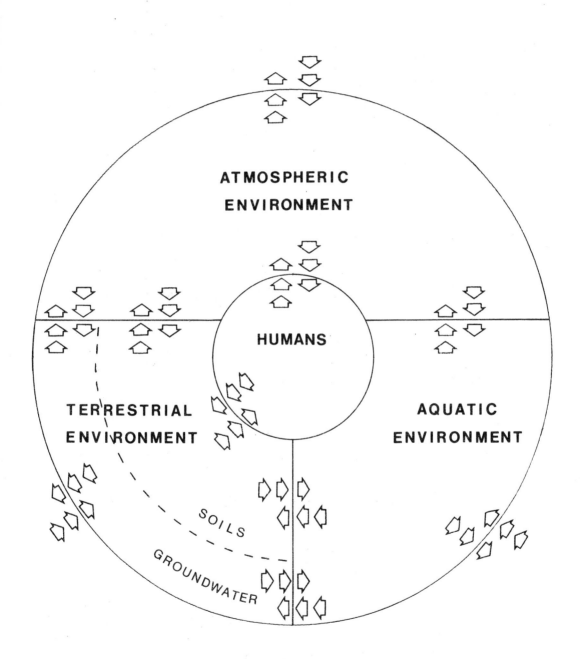

position to define the scope of the environmental issues and to develop practical remedial solutions.

The diagram can most effectively be summarized as "everything is connected to everything else". As the Phase I environmental review clearly illustrates, human influences are dominant in all aspects of the environment of the East Bayfront/Port Industrial Area. The resulting environmental conditions affect human health and quality of life.

The diagram also includes relationships between the study area and its regional context. The information reviewed during Phase I identified some of the contributions to the study area from outside (e.g., pollution of air and water) and some of the influences of the study area on adjacent neighbourhoods (e.g., odours from industrial activities).

To illustrate the kinds of interactions inherent in the diagram, examples of some of the potential ecosystem links identified, but not studied, during the Phase I review include:

- transfer of contaminants from soils/groundwater to ambient air in windblown dust and soil;

- transfer of contaminants from soils/groundwater to buildings, affecting indoor air quality;

- movement of contaminants from groundwater to the lake;

- deposition of airborne contaminants (e.g., lead, salt) to soils;

- food-chain contamination resulting in accumulation of toxics in wildlife;

- spatial links of wildlife habitats: the waterfront and the Don Valley.

IN CONCLUSION

The Phase I review of existing information about the environmental conditions of the East Bayfront/Port Industrial

Area has given us a preliminary indication of the nature and extent of environmental problems there. It has also shown the value of both built heritage and natural heritage, which can enrich future uses.

Our examination of the legislative framework for environmental protection and rehabilitation made clear that it is complex and in a state of flux. It comprises statutes, regulations, guidelines, and policies of the federal government, the provincial government, and the municipalities. In many cases, environmental protection depends on guidelines or objectives rather than enforceable regulations.

Many important gaps in our knowledge of the environment of the study area were identified. In response, a number of options for Phase II research have been proposed, focused on an ecosystem approach. The purpose of the Phase II research will be to provide a better understanding of the environmental conditions of the area, as a basis for future decisions about environmental remediation, protection, and enhancement.

Although the focus of the environmental audit is a small part of the Toronto waterfront, it has symbolic importance because of the existing and potential relationships between it and the larger environment. The area is part of a watershed, part of an airshed, a home and migration stop-over for wildlife. The strategic location of the East Bayfront/Port Industrial Area on the waterfront and at the mouth of the Don River offers the opportunity to show how environmental protection and enhancement can become part of existing and future uses and contribute to a healthier community.

COMMISSION REPORTS AND WORKING PAPERS

Reports and working papers published by the Royal Commission on the Future of the Toronto Waterfront are available in both English and French. Publications may be obtained by contacting Andrea G. Short, Publications Co–ordinator, at the Royal Commission on the Future of the Toronto Waterfront, 207 Queen's Quay West, 5th Floor, P.O. Box 4111, Station A, Toronto, Ontario M5W 2V4.

Requests for information or comments about the content of the Commission's reports may be directed to Beverly Morley, Director of Community Relations.

1. *Environment and Health: Issues on the Toronto Waterfront.* Royal Commission on the Future of the Toronto Waterfront. Environment and Health Work Group. ISBN 0–662–16539–2. DSS cat. no. Z1–1988/1–41–1E

2. *Housing and Neighbourhoods: The Liveable Waterfront.* Royal Commission on the Future of the Toronto Waterfront. Housing and Neighbourhoods Work Group. ISBN 0–662–16936–0. DSS cat. no. Z1–1988/1–41–2E

3. *Access and Movement*: Royal Commission on the Future of the Toronto Waterfront. Access and Movement Work Group. ISBN 0–662–16937–9. DSS cat. no. Z1–1988/1–41–3E

4. *Parks, Pleasures, and Public Amenities.* Royal Commission on the Future of the Toronto Waterfront. Parks, Pleasures, and Public Amenities Work Group. ISBN 0–662–16936–0. DSS cat. no. Z1–1988/1–41–4E

5. *Jobs, Opportunities, and Economic Growth.* Royal Commission on the Future of the Toronto Waterfront. Jobs, Opportunities and Economic Growth Work Group. ISBN 0–662–16939–5. DSS cat. no. Z1–1988/1–41–5E

6. *Persistence and Change: Waterfront Issues and the Board of Toronto Harbour Commissioners.* Royal Commission on the

Future of the Toronto Waterfront. Steering Committee on Matters Relating to the Board of Toronto Harbour Commissioners. ISBN 0–662–16966–2. DSS cat. no. Z1–1988/1–41–6E

7. *The Future of the Toronto Island Airport: The Issues*. Royal Commission on the Future of the Toronto Waterfront. ISBN 0–662–17067–9. DSS cat. no. Z1–1988/1–41–7E

8. *A Green Strategy for the Greater Toronto Waterfront: Background and Issues*. Ron Reid, Rob Lockhart, and Bob Woodburn. Royal Commission on the Future of the Toronto Waterfront. ISBN 0–662–17671–5. DSS cat. no. Z1–1988/1–41–8E

9. *Waterfront Transportation in the Context of Regional Transportation: Background and Issues*. Neal A. Irwin, and F. Shane Foreman. Royal Commission on the Future of the Toronto Waterfront. ISBN 0–662–17730–4. DSS cat no. Z1–1988/1–52–2E

Interim Report August 1989. Royal Commission on the Future of the Toronto Waterfront. ISBN 0–662–17215–9. DSS cat. no. Z1–1988/1E

Working Papers

A Selected Bibliography on Toronto's Port and Waterfront
CAT Z1–1988/1–42–1E
ISBN 0–662–17596–4

An Index to the First Interim Report
CAT Z1–1988/1–42–2E
ISBN 0–662–17597–2

Urban Waterfront Industry: Planning and Developing Green Enterprise for the 21st Century; a Report of the Symposium, November 16, 1989
CAT Z1–1988/1–52–1E
ISBN 0–662–17640–5